Reading for Academic Success

Reading for Academic Success

Powerful
Strategies
for Struggling,
Average,
and
Advanced
Readers,
Grades 7-12

Richard W. Strong
Matthew J. Perini

Harvey F. Silver
Gregory M. Tuculescu

CORWIN PRESS, INC.
A Sage Publications Company
Thousand Oaks, California

For information:

Corwin Press, Inc.
A Sage Publications Company
2455 Teller Road
Thousand Oaks, California 91320
E-mail: order@corwinpress.com

Sage Publications Ltd.
6 Bonhill Street
London EC2A 4PU
United Kingdom

Sage Publications India Pvt. Ltd.
M-32 Market
Greater Kailash I
New Delhi 110 048 India

Printed in the United States of America

Library of Congress Cataloging-in-Publication Data

Reading for academic success: Powerful strategies for struggling, average, and advanced readers, grades 7-12 / by Richard W. Strong ... [et al.].
    p. cm.
  Includes bibliographical references and index.
  ISBN 0-7619-7833-X (c) — ISBN 0-7619-7834-8 (p)
  1. Reading (Secondary) 2. Reading comprehension. 3. Study skills.   I. Strong, Richard W., 1946-
  LB1632 .R356 2002
  428.4′071′2—dc21

                                  2001006313

This book is printed on acid-free paper.

02 03 04 05 06 07 7 6 5 4 3 2 1

Acquisitions Editor: Rachel Livsey
Editorial Assistant: Phyllis Cappello
Production Editor: Olivia Weber
Typesetter/Designer: Rebecca Evans/Lynn Miyata
Copy Editor: Marilyn Power Scott
Indexer: Teri Greenberg
Cover Designer: Michael Dubowe

Contents

■ ■

Preface: The A+ Reader

■ ■

Chances are good that if you purchased this book, you're an educator. But the chances are even better that you're a reader. Nonreaders buy few books, rarely visit libraries, and are much more likely to go online to play video games than they are to check out the latest research on the human genome project or participate in a chat room discussion on the achievements of Satchel Paige or the tragedy of Manzanar.

This is a book about how you can turn average or below-average readers in secondary school into thoughtful, high-achieving readers—readers, like yourself, who can find and remember the information they need, reason out the implications of powerful and challenging ideas, and feel at home in libraries and bookstores, both virtual and real.

But I'm Not a Reading Teacher! Why Does Reading Matter to Me?

This book is not just for reading teachers. It is not even just for teachers. It is for any secondary educator who is concerned with student achievement and success in the Information Age. Whether you teach English, Math, Social Studies, Science, or any other subject; whether you work with average, advanced, or special-needs students or, as is most likely, a combination of all three; whether you're a principal, director of curriculum, professional development specialist, or school leader; whether you are about to enter the education profession, or have twenty-five years of service under your belt, reading is important. We can think of three reasons why:

1. Reading is an essential skill in our culture. Pretend you are a parent (if you already are one, this should be easy). You are faced with a choice between two high schools. One promises that by the end of senior year, your child will know the three stages of cellular respiration and the facts of the Nullification Crisis. The other school guarantees that your child will be able to read and understand any text he or she encounters in college and in life, no matter how difficult. Which school would you choose?

2. *Reading is a skill we count on.* No amount of lectures, videos, or inquiries will permit you to cover all the essential material in your discipline. As educators, we rely on students' abilities to learn through reading. Textbooks, articles, literature, online resources, primary documents, lab manuals—all of these and many other resources serve as the foundation for powerful teaching and learning. This means that students who can't read at a high level of proficiency are missing a vital piece in the learning puzzle.

3. *Reading is thinking.* Well-written texts model good thinking. Through reading, essential learning and thinking strategies, such as gathering evidence, organizing ideas, forming images, drawing conclusions, and raising questions, are regularly modeled, practiced, and internalized. Thus, thoughtful readers become thoughtful problem solvers—and better students.

How many more reasons can you imagine to make good reading a central part of your curriculum?

Can We Really Improve Reading in Secondary School?

The answer is unequivocally yes. But twenty years ago, it wasn't so easy to be so unequivocal. Why? Because, for decades, research on reading focused almost exclusively on the difficulties readers faced. You might say this research was more concerned with what readers could not do than with what they could do—with readers' disabilities rather than their abilities. Then, in the late 1970s and early 1980s, reading research took a sharp turn in a different direction. Under the leadership of researchers such as Robert Tierney, P. David Pearson, Ruth Garner, James Cunningham, Annemarie Palinscar, Ann Brown, and others, reading research began to focus on the mental activity of proficient readers. What these and other researchers asked themselves was this: What do good and great readers do with their minds while reading that makes them more successful than their peers? What they found was that good and great readers shared five characteristics that made them A+ rather than C+ readers:

- A+ readers know how to organize ideas and information to fit the task at hand.

- A+ readers know how to use questions to filter out the most important information and to clarify points of confusion.

- A+ readers know how to use their imagination to make predictions, draw inferences, and create pictures that mirror important concepts in the text.

- A+ readers know how to use conversation, dialogue, and retelling to deepen their understanding of the texts they read.

- A+ readers recognize when their understanding of texts is confused or mistaken and use strategies to repair their comprehension.

Armed with this new vision of the talents and skills employed by successful readers, teachers and researchers alike began to craft instruction in these skills into strategies teachers could use to improve reading while continuing to teach their specific content. And, because of the new research base behind them—because the focus was on ability rather than disability—the strategies worked. Weaker readers grew stronger. C+ students earned more A's.

How This Book Is Organized

This book is a collection of the strategies that have emerged from the proficient-reader research. Each chapter is focused on a specific reading challenge students face in secondary school and the strategies that will help them meet that challenge.

- *Chapter 1* focuses on that most pervasive and often difficult source of information in secondary school: *the textbook*.

- *Chapter 2* turns our attention to the importance of *note making* as a tool for focusing attention and building reading comprehension.

- *Chapter 3* is designed to help students learn how to manage and master the wealth and variety of *vocabulary* that they confront in all content areas.

- *Chapter 4* contains strategies that develop students' abilities to read beyond the information given, to move from the gist to deeper, more *inferential reading*.

- *Chapter 5* asks, How can students become better and more thoughtful readers by tapping into the power of *questions*?

- *Chapter 6* demonstrates how to use *informal writing and journals* to keep readers active, reflective, and connected to their own interests and experiences.

- *Chapter 7* looks at students' individual *reading styles* and helps teachers to differentiate and individualize teaching and learning so that all students receive the reading instruction they need and deserve.

In addition to the strategies, each chapter contains two other special features: *Applications to Specific Content Areas*, which shows how to vary and adapt the strategies to the demands of different disciplines, and *Strategies for Struggling Readers*, which provides tips and tools for working with our weakest readers in heterogeneous classrooms or special-needs settings. Many of the strategies come with full-page reproducibles, named *Resources*, to facilitate classroom lessons; we encourage you to copy, use, and modify them to best suit your needs.

We all want our students to learn. And we all know the importance of reading to both academic and lifelong learning. The strategies and tools within these pages will help you nurture the skills your students will need to become confident, thoughtful, A+ readers.

About the Authors

■ ■

Richard W. Strong is Vice President of Silver Strong & Associates and has served as a trainer-consultant to hundreds of school districts around the world. As cofounder of the Institute for Community and Difference, Richard has been studying democratic teaching practices in public and private schools for more than ten years. He has written and developed numerous educational books and products, including *Questioning Styles and Strategies* and the *Teaching Strategies Video Library*.

Harvey F. Silver, President of Silver Strong & Associates, was recently named as one of the 100 most influential teachers in the United States. He is the coauthor of numerous books for educators, including *Teaching Styles and Strategies*, currently being used in the Master of Arts in Teaching programs at fourteen colleges and universities. He is a member of the advisory board of the International Creative and Innovative Thinking Association.

Matthew J. Perini, Director of Publishing at Silver Strong & Associates, has authored curriculum guides, articles, and research studies on a wide range of topics, including learning styles, multiple intelligences, and effective teaching practices.

Strong, Silver, and Perini have recently collaborated on *Discovering Nonfiction: 25 Powerful Teaching Strategies, Grades 2-6; So Each May Learn: Integrating Learning Styles and Multiple Intelligences;* and *Teaching What Matters Most: Standards and Strategies for Raising Student Achievement*.

Gregory M. Tuculescu is a writer, editor, and researcher for Silver Strong & Associates who has coauthored several books in *The Teaching Strategies Library*. He has also authored several curriculum guides, including *A Thinker's Guide to Ancient Egypt*.

To Peta,
without whose patience and hard work this book
would have remained scribble and scrawl.

CHAPTER 1

The Challenge of Textbook Reading

```
                    ┌─────────────────────┐
                    │   The Challenge of  │
                    │   Textbook Reading  │
                    └─────────────────────┘
```

- The Challenge of Textbook Reading
  - Strategies for Developing Effective Textbook Readers
    - Text Structure
      - Visual Organizers
    - Peer Reading
      - Collaborative Summarizing
    - Questioning the Author
  - Applications to Specific Content Areas
    - How Text Structures Differ From One Content Area to Another
    - Reading Charts, Maps, Graphs, and Tables in Science and Social Studies
  - Strategies for Struggling Readers
    - Helping Students Overcome Prereading Problems
    - Helping Students Overcome During-Reading Problems
    - Helping Students Overcome Post-Reading Problems

Like it or not, textbooks are here to stay. Even as technology changes the nature of nonfiction reading into a multisensory, multitext experience, the textbook—that single, hardbound, seemingly complete container of a year's worth of content—remains a constant. In fact, recent studies show that more than two-thirds of all instruction is structured or guided by textbooks (Woodward & Elliott, 1990). Even if we chose to reject textbooks completely—cast them aside as biased, or poorly written, or demotivating—it turns out that we would be doing our students a disservice in preparing them for college, where the first-year student is asked to read, on average, eighty pages per class per week, with most of the load coming from textbooks (Carson, Chase, Gibson, & Hargrove, 1992). In these case study college classes, it was the implicit expectation of the professors that students would be able to organize textbook information effectively so it could be used later. Add to this all the technical manuals, how-to resources, and informational material we read at work, at home, and online, and the importance of textbook reading becomes even clearer. Obviously, with so much riding on their futures, students need to become effective and strategic textbook readers.

Overcoming the Image of the Textbook

Do you remember your own experiences with textbooks when you were a student? For most of us, these experiences were neither pleasant nor particularly memorable. Our textbooks contained information—lots of information—and it was expected that we would be able to remember at least some of this information for tests and quizzes. But for some of us, the textbook experience was far worse than simply prosaic; textbooks were nightmares of information that never stopped coming. Trying to differentiate the important information from the not-so-important information, attempting to make sense of tables and diagrams that were sandwiched into text, keeping track of all the new vocabulary words, doing our best to thwart boredom and lagging attention spans—these are the associations many of us and many of our students have.

Thus, a big part of teaching students the skills involved in textbook reading lies in overcoming their perceptions of the textbook. For we can be certain that if our own associations of textbooks are negative, yet we continue to use them in roughly the same way that our teachers did, then our students are similarly bored and frustrated in our classrooms. In general, overcoming the image of the textbook means developing a curriculum that

- Uses the textbook to enrich teaching and learning but does not rely on it to drive teaching and learning

- Balances textbook reading with other sources of information, including primary documents, periodical and journal articles, and texts that provide different perspectives

- Incorporates, when possible, Internet- or technology-based reading and research that, through its plurality of media, enriches and enlivens the classroom while it develops essential research and information-management skills

- Encourages students to read the textbook critically, discussing potential biases, poorly written passages, and difficulties in understanding

From the standpoint of instruction, two critical shifts are required to turn students into successful textbook readers:

1. Because textbook reading is so often difficult for students, the teacher should model and teach the skills and strategies students will need to address specific kinds of reading difficulties.

2. Because students will need to apply these skills throughout their academic and vocational careers, the teacher should promote student independence and growth by gradually shifting responsibility for these skills and strategies to students.

Why Are Textbooks Hard to Read?

Four commonly cited answers to this question follow:

1. Text structure. Often, the overriding pattern used to arrange the part-to-whole or big-idea-to-subtopic relationships is invisible to students. Lacking a big picture to work from makes it unlikely that students will be able to extract the essential information from their reading.

2. Information overload. Textbook prose is saturated with information: facts, names, equations, battles, chemical processes, figures, diagrams, charts, old concepts, new concepts, familiar vocabulary, unfamiliar vocabulary. Without a strategic approach for managing this flood of information, many students lose their way through the text as well as their motivation to keep pushing forward.

3. The "authority" of the textbook. Despite the shortcomings of textbooks, most students believe that the information and writing inside them are unassailable. This perceived authority of the textbook can disarm students, turning their questions into passive nods of acceptance. It is almost as if textbooks somehow hide the fact that they—like all texts—are written by people who can hold biases, write poorly and unclearly, and leave out important information and whose methods of presenting information must be actively questioned by readers. Thus, turning students into active textbook readers means helping them conduct critical examinations of their textbooks.

4. New vocabulary and concepts that are disconnected from experience and prior knowledge. Countless studies of both proficient and poor readers show that the ability to integrate the new with the old, to tap into prior knowledge and to use it to illuminate new ideas, is a key to reading well. Textbooks, however, make this skill especially difficult because they contain so much information that, in many cases, seems to make no connection to what the students already know. The preponderance of new concepts and new vocabulary requires students to look for other ways to make their reading meaningful.

The next section of this chapter contains a set of strategies designed to help students overcome each of these difficulties. (Because vocabulary is such a common and pervasive issue in all secondary classrooms, we have devoted a separate chapter to managing and mastering vocabulary.)

Text Structure and Visual Organizers help students to recognize common text patterns and graphically arrange important information.

Peer Reading and Collaborative Summarizing teach students how to manage large amounts of information, discriminate between essential and nonessential information, and condense reading into powerful summaries.

Questioning the Author teaches students how to "interrogate" a text and construct meaningful interpretations of textbook passages and chapters.

After the strategies, you will find a section titled *Applications to Specific Content Areas*, which highlights the issues of discipline-specific text structures and the preponderance of graphics in social studies and science. Last, in a section titled *Strategies for Struggling Readers*, you will find tips, suggestions, and strategic approaches to assisting readers before, during, and after reading.

Strategies for Developing Effective Textbook Readers

Text Structure and Visual Organizers

Overview

A common impediment to textbook readers is the inability to "see" a text's structure. Without understanding the underlying pattern, students have trouble understanding how information is connected, and the text can become a meaningless stew. This strategy teaches students how to identify text structure and use visual organizers to expose the critical relationships within a reading.

Steps in Implementation

1. Explain and model how to use a graphic organizer to record essential information from a text. Show students how to identify text structure and choose visual organizers that complement the text structure.

2. Distribute copies of the sample organizer to each student in the class (reproducible versions of the most common organizer structures are included at the end of this strategy). Address student questions on the use of the organizer.

3. Allow students time to read and record information on their organizers. Observe students' progress, and help those who may be having difficulty.

4. When students have finished, conduct a review session with the whole class to make sure all students have recorded the essential information from the reading and have used the organizers correctly.

5. Assign students a culminating or processing activity that will allow them to use their organizers. For example, you could ask students to write an essay, create and explain a metaphor, create a time line, or build a model.

6. Guide students toward selecting (or even designing) organizers to complement any text structure they may encounter. The ultimate goal of the strategy is for students to identify text structure and use organizers independently.

Strategy in the Classroom

Here's an example of this strategy in action: Robert Gilman has begun a unit on Ancient Greece with his ninth-grade World History class. He wants his students to understand the series of events that led to the Golden Age of Athens, a period that helped shape the Western world.

Robert says,

> Some people see history as isolated events occurring at a certain time in a certain place. A good historian, however, knows that events never occur in isolation but are part of a sequence of events that shape history. The next section in our book deals with a series of events known as the Persian Wars that eventually led to the Golden Age of Athens. As you read, I want you to pay particular attention to how events build upon one another to create the picture of an age.

Robert then distributes the sequence organizers the students will use to record the key events and ideas during their reading (see Figure 1.1). While his students work, Robert walks around the room observing them, making sure they understand how to use the organizer to extract the essential information from the text. When the students are finished, he conducts a review of key ideas and events on the board. Once the review is complete, Robert asks his students to use their organizers to write a short essay that examines the question, "Would the Golden Age of Athens have happened without the Persian Wars?"

Here's another example: In her biology class, Marcy Jackson has decided to use a topic organizer to help her students understand and remember the parts and functions of a cell. She begins by giving her students a quick introductory lecture on the concept of the cell, relating its parts and functions to the parts and

Figure 1.1. The Golden Age of Athens

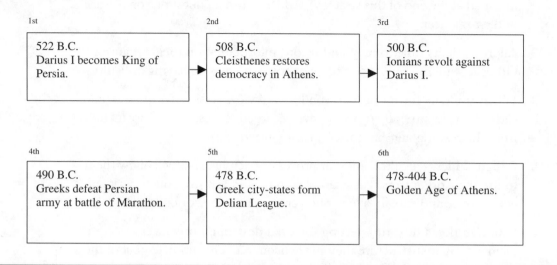

functions of the human body. She explains to her students that they will be reading a section in their book that is filled with information, most of which will be unfamiliar to them.

Marcy explains:

> It's easy to feel overwhelmed by all the information that you are going to find in this section. There will be plenty of new vocabulary that you've probably never come across before. I would like all of you to know the parts and functions of a cell by the end of this unit, but I also want you to understand how these parts affect each other and interact. I think if you know how a cell works instead of simply memorizing its parts, your understanding will be comprehensive.

Marcy then goes on to show her students how to use a topic organizer to show hierarchical relationships and connections between terms and ideas (see Figure 1.2). As her students work, she circulates through the room helping those who have difficulty using the organizer or picking out key ideas. When they have finished, she conducts a class review to make sure everyone's organizer has all the essential information. As a culminating activity, Marcy asks her students to use their organizers to explore the metaphor How is a cell like a city? Students relate parts of the cell to parts or departments in a city and justify their metaphors with detailed explanations.

Why the Strategy Works (What the Research Says)

Textbooks are designed to hold vast amounts of information, often covering entire disciplines, such as biology, or thousands of years of Western history in a

Figure 1.2. The Cell

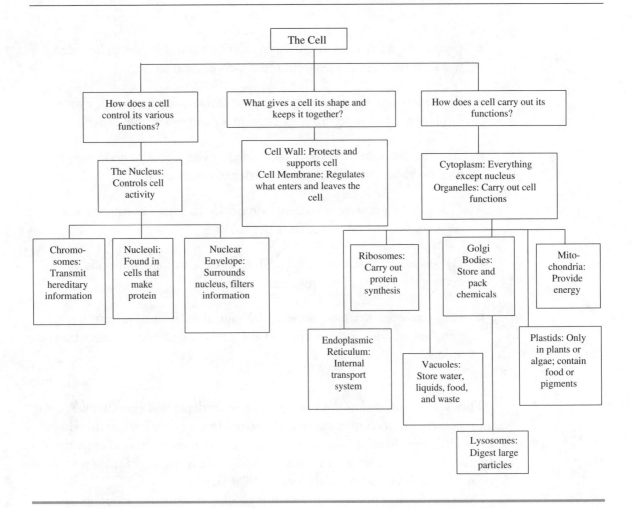

single volume. In an effort to make an overwhelming amount of information manageable and the content more accessible, textbook editors and nonfiction writers use various text structures. Yet for many students, especially average and struggling students, these structures are invisible. Think of this problem as the difference between trying to find a knife in a junk drawer versus trying to find a knife in an organized silverware drawer. To the student who can't see text structure, every text looks like a junk drawer.

Compounding this problem is the fact that most students are exposed to the structure of fiction texts and narrative in elementary grades, but they get little training in nonfiction structures. This lack of familiarity with nonfiction structures makes seeing organizational patterns doubly difficult. Addressing this problem means helping students learn to see how texts are organized and how to extract the essential information from each type of structure (Just & Carpenter, 1987).

Text structure can change any number of times in a given reading, yet most structures fall into six basic formats:

- *Comparison structures* examine the similarities and differences between two or more events, ideas, concepts, people, and so on.

- *Time line or sequence structures* present the chronological order of events or place a list of procedures or steps in a comprehensible order.

- *Topic description structures* relate facts, ideas, events, and so on in simple lists, one after the other, often in order of importance.

- *Cycle structures* represent patterns or trends in ideas, events, or concepts that often end where they began.

- *Problem-solution structures* set up problems, explain their solutions, and discuss the effects of the solution.

- *Cause-and-effect structures* present the causal relationship between a given event, idea, or concept and the events, ideas, or concepts that follow.

These are by no means the only structures students will encounter. A more comprehensive list of content-specific text structures appears later in this chapter. The six structures listed, however, are those most commonly found in textbooks today. For this reason, we have created reproducible organizers for each of these structures, which you'll find at the end of this section.

Once the teacher has modeled each type of text structure, students can follow the pattern of organization to extract important ideas, concepts, and events. To do this well, students must be taught to look for cues or signal words that alert readers to the structure. For example, in a text presenting a sequence of events or steps, students may find many of the following words: first, second, third, finally, last, now, then, next, while. (See reproducible sample organizers for signal words associated with each type of structure.) Of course, practice in identifying different structures and whole-class discussions on problems and insights will help students gain independence.

Students who can identify text structure can then use visual organizers that mirror that structure to record essential information they take from the text. According to Marzano, Gaddy, and Dean (2000), visual organizers make information memorable by presenting it in both linguistic and nonlinguistic modes. In other words, information is both visually structured according to the pattern of the organizer and concisely condensed into words for deep comprehension and easier memorization. Resources 1.1 through 1.6 are reproducible examples of various organizers.

Resource 1.1. Comparison Organizer

Name:_____

Comparison Organizer _____

Differences	**Differences**

Similarities

Signal words: on one hand, similarly, but, then, either … or

Resource 1.2. Sequence Organizer

Name:_____

Sequence Organizer

First	Second	Third

Fourth	Fifth	Sixth

Signal words: now, then, first, second, next, finally, while

Resource 1.3. Topic Description Organizer

Name:_____

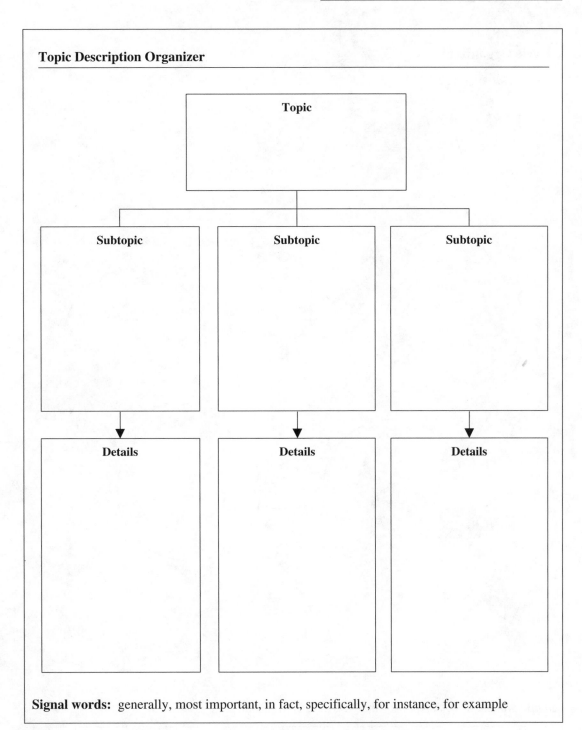

Topic Description Organizer

Topic

Subtopic

Subtopic

Subtopic

Details

Details

Details

Signal words: generally, most important, in fact, specifically, for instance, for example

Resource 1.4. Cycle Organizer

Name: _____

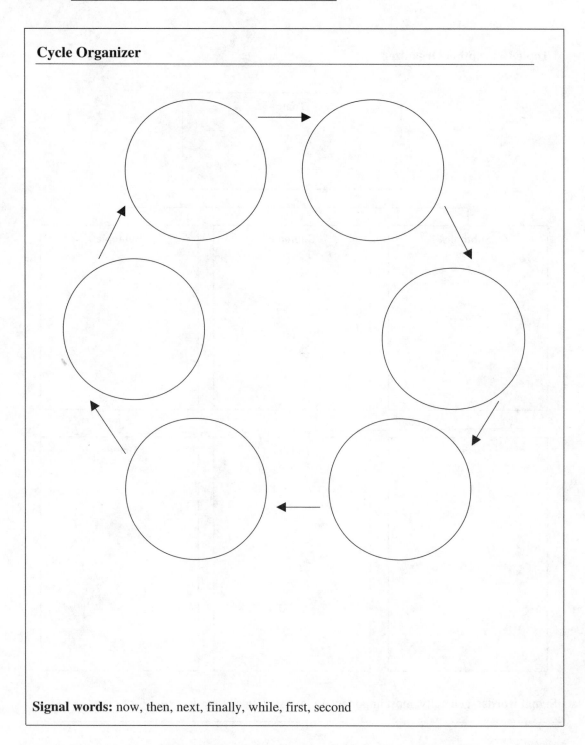

Cycle Organizer

Signal words: now, then, next, finally, while, first, second

Resource 1.5. Problem-Solution Organizer

Name:_____

Problem/Solution Organizer
_____

Problem	Solution	Effect

Signal words: since, as a result, this led to, because, so, if … then

Resource 1.6. Cause-Effect Organizer

Name:_____

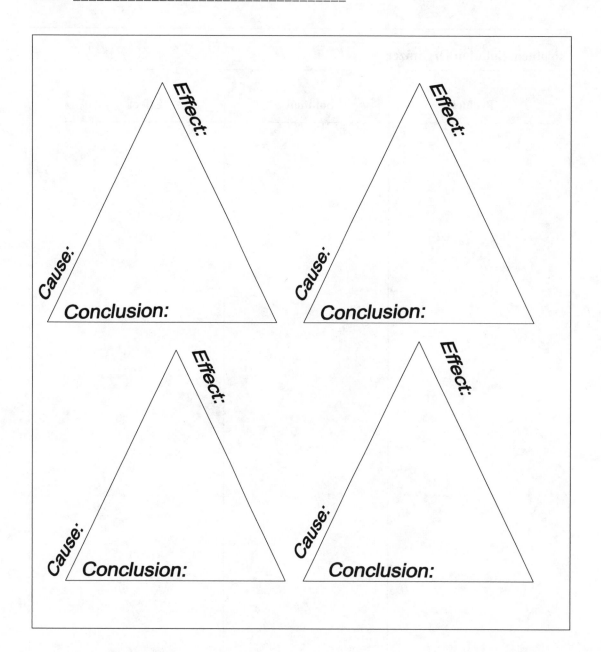

Peer Reading

Overview

Because textbooks are so densely packed with information, many students feel overwhelmed, lost in a sea of words and disconnected ideas. *Peer Reading* is a partnering technique that teaches students how to break down a reading into manageable chunks, use questions to focus on essential information, and distill a reading into a concise summary.

Steps in Implementation

1. Select a reading and break it down into three or four smaller sections. Create questions for each section that focus student reading toward important information and record them on the Peer Reading Coaching Sheet (a sample Peer Reading Coaching Sheet is shown in the upcoming classroom example).

2. Pair students up, and assign each member of each pair a letter, A or B. Explain that both students will read each section and then will alternate roles as coach and oral summarizer (Reader A will use his or her notes to coach Reader B to a complete summary of the section and vice versa).

3. Have students continue to reverse roles as coach and summarizer until all questions on the Peer Reading Coaching Sheet are answered.

4. Ask students to work in their pairs to summarize the entire reading using their notes and marked texts.

5. As students become comfortable with Peer Reading, encourage them to chunk and question on their own, as a way of managing textual overload.

How the Strategy Works in the Classroom

In Jerry Kendal's tenth-grade psychology class, students have been studying human development. His students are about to read a section in their textbooks about Piaget's theories of childhood development. Based on the last writing assignment, Jerry realizes that his students are having trouble extracting essential information from their textbooks. In response, he has decided to use Peer Reading to slow down the reading process of his students so they can gain greater control over the information. He splits a four-page passage on Piaget into four readings of relatively equal length. He asks his students to pair up and assigns each member of each pair either a letter A or B. Jerry then introduces the class to the coaching sheet they will use to complete the reading (see Figure 1.3).

Student pair Paul and Jenny begin by reading the first passage independently. As they read, both students use the summarizing questions on their coaching sheets to take notes and record what they believe to be central ideas and important facts or details. They also note any new vocabulary they may encounter. When both students have finished the passage, Paul (Reader A) takes

Figure 1.3. Peer Reading Coaching Sheet

Peer Reading Coaching Sheet

Section 1 questions (Reader A)

1. According to Piaget, where do the roots of knowledge lie?

2. What are the first two stages of childhood development?

Section 2 questions (Reader B)

1. What are the last two stages of development?

2. Why is it important that children "transcend egocentrism"?

Section 3 questions (Reader A)

1. What can adolescents in the last stage of development do that younger children cannot?

2. How are assimilation and accommodation related?

Section 4 questions (Reader B)

1. What are the major criticisms of Piaget's theory?

2. What do experts consider to be Piaget's greatest contribution to developmental psychology?

---

a moment to look over his marked passage and then turns the copy over, while Jenny (Reader B) uses her marked passage to coach Paul to complete answers to the questions under "Section 1" on the Peer Reading Coaching Sheet:

> Jenny: OK. Ready?

> Paul: Ready.

Jenny: Question one: According to Piaget, where do the roots of knowledge lie?

Paul: OK, well, Piaget was interested in how a child's experiences shape his development, so the roots of knowledge lie in a child's interaction with the world around him.

Jenny: Good, but there's a simple answer.

Paul: OK, wait . . . uh, was this near the beginning of the passage?

Jenny: Yup.

Paul: Well, they focused quite a bit on action initially . . . that's it, action! The roots of knowledge, according to Piaget, lie in action!

Jenny: Good job! Question two . . .

Once Paul has finished answering the questions under "Section 1," he and Jenny continue on to the second reading. This time, their roles are reversed. Paul (Reader A) becomes the coach, while Jenny (Reader B) turns over her text to answer the questions for Section 2. The partners continue this process for Sections 3 and 4, each time switching roles, until all the questions on the Peer Reading Coaching Sheet have been answered.

Once all the questions have been answered, Paul and Jenny look over their answers to the questions on the coaching sheet and work together to create a summary of Piaget's four stages of cognitive development. Throughout this process, Jerry walks around the room observing his students. He pays special attention to any problems students encounter in trying to answer questions or in creating a summary. Over the next month, as students learn about social development in children, Jerry will teach students how to use this process on their own by chunking the text and asking themselves summarizing questions to determine what is essential information in their reading.

Why the Strategy Works (What the Research Says)

Summarizing is such an old practice that the teaching of the method has yet to catch up with modern educational theory. Traditionally, when a teacher engages a student in a summarizing activity, the expectation is that the student will be able to ignore unnecessary ideas and details, form a more generalized concept, and pick out main ideas or topic sentences from a reading.

The problems with this method of teaching become apparent when we examine the assumed skills these tasks take for granted. Peter Afflerbach and Peter H. Johnston (1986) keenly note that when teachers ask a student to delete unimportant information, they are assuming the student already knows how to extract only the essential information.

Following the findings of research showing how questions help readers focus on essential information and manage longer readings (Just & Carpenter, 1987; Wood, 1986), Silver, Hanson, Strong, and Schwartz (1996) developed the Peer

Reading strategy. This method of reading and summarizing brings the following advantages to the students' learning experience:

- Through oral summary and the support of a coach, students are involved in deep processing of the content.

- The task of summarizing is structured by the use of coaching questions that point students toward essential information.

- Information is extracted from the text in a number of ways, including coaching, taking notes, answering questions, and writing a collaborative summary.

- Students work toward creating their own coaching questions and developing autonomy with the process so they can use the strategy as an independent research tool.

Resource 1.7 shows a sample blank, reproducible Peer Reading coaching sheet.

Collaborative Summarizing: Helping Students Build More Powerful Summaries

Some students may have trouble creating effective summaries, even after they have practiced using Peer Reading. Collaborative Summarizing (Silver, Strong, & Perini, 2001) is a strategy that will help them build confidence and independence with this vital skill. To use Collaborative Summarizing in your classroom, distribute summary sheets (see Resource 1.8) and proceed through the following six steps.

1. Ask students to list three to five ideas that they feel are the most important in the reading.

2. Have students pair up and review the rules for peer negotiation:
   a. You must use textual evidence to show why an idea is important.
   b. Do not jump to simple solutions.
   c. This is not a contest of wills, so avoid win-lose situations.

   Ask students to come to an agreement on the three to five most important ideas, using the foregoing rules.

3. Allow each student pair to meet with another pair to renegotiate their list of ideas. Explain that this final list will be the basis for their summary, so they should arrange it in a way that will make sense when written out. For example, one student group created this list for a reading on the role of geometry in Renaissance art:

Resource 1.7. Sample Peer Reading Coaching Sheet

Peer Reading Coaching Sheet
Section 1 questions (Reader A)
Section 2 questions (Reader B)
Section 3 questions (Reader A)
Section 4 questions (Reader B)

    a. Unlike Medieval artists, Renaissance artists wanted to paint objects realistically and accurately.

    b. Many Renaissance artists turned to geometry to help them paint more realistically.

    c. They discovered that parallel lines running directly away from the viewer come together at a *vanishing point* on the horizon.

    d. They used this knowledge to create a three-dimensional effect called *perspective*.

    e. Raphael, Leonardo da Vinci, and Albrecht Dürer all relied on perspective to create their most famous paintings.

4. Ask students to use their final lists to write their summaries individually.

5. Have each original team of four meet with another team of four. Students read and discuss their summaries, then develop a set of criteria for creating powerful summaries. Students share and refine these criteria through whole-class discussion.

6. Over the course of the year, students refer to these criteria to help them create effective summaries of different texts.

A sample reproducible Collaborative Summarizing worksheet is shown in Resource 1.8.

Questioning the Author

Overview

It is not uncommon for students to view textbooks as infallible sources of information. This view, however, fosters a passive approach to reading, where learning is not constructed by the reader and where information is rarely questioned. The strategy called Questioning the Author seeks to make students active participants in constructing meaning and critiquing the way information is presented in textbooks.

Steps in Implementation

1. Explain to students that an author's meaning in a text is not always easy to understand and that authors can sometimes be unclear or write poorly.

2. Have students read a selected text. At critical points during the reading, stop to pose initiating queries that will spark group discussion, such as, "What is the author trying to say here?" or "What does the author want us to understand in this section?"

3. Guide discussion by delving more deeply into the text's meaning or pointing out missing information by posing follow-up queries, such as, "Does the author fully support this statement?" "How does this compare with

Resource 1.8. Collaborative Summarizing Worksheet

Collaborative Summarizing Worksheet

Topic:_____

My key ideas:	My partner's key ideas:
Our key ideas:	Their key ideas:

What we all agreed on:

Criteria for Powerful Summaries:

what the author said before?" "Is the reason for this explained in the text?"

4. Allow students time to reflect on and discuss the meaning of the text and the process of Questioning the Author.

How the Strategy Works in the Classroom

Alison Quipac's U.S. History I class is studying the Civil War. Much of the information they have gathered has come from their textbooks, supplementary readings provided by Alison, and documentaries. Alison's students are about to read a passage in their textbooks about the Emancipation Proclamation, which she feels is unclear. Alison says,

> I know I've been having you all read your textbooks at home for the past few weeks, but today, I'd like to try something a little different. We're going to read a passage on the Emancipation Proclamation together, aloud. As we read, I want you to think about what the authors are trying to say and how they are saying it.

Alison then begins to read the passage aloud with her students. She pauses several times during the reading to pose questions that go beyond the literal content of the passage to get at information the authors may have left out or neglected. She sparks discussion in the following manner:

> Alison: OK. Let's pause for a moment. What are the authors trying to say here?
>
> Kareem: They say Lincoln declared that slaves would be free in the South by January 1, 1863.
>
> Alison: Did the authors say slaves would be free in "the South" or were they more specific?
>
> Kareem: They said slaves would be freed in territories controlled by the rebels.
>
> Alison: OK. Kareem has led us to a key phrase here, "territories controlled by the rebels." Why do the authors use this phrase as opposed to just saying "the South"? Brendan?
>
> Brendan: Well, uh, I think it's because Union troops controlled areas of the South like, uh, the authors mention Maryland, Missouri, and Kentucky.
>
> Alison: So Brendan is saying that the North actually controlled areas of the South, but Kareem pointed out that Lincoln declared that slaves would be free in rebel-controlled territories in the South by January 1, 1863. So would Lincoln have been able to enforce that proclamation in rebel-controlled territories? Tony?

Tony: No.

Alison: Did the authors of the textbook make that clear? Melissa?

Melissa: Well, not exactly. I mean, they made it sound like the Emancipation Proclamation was, like, a law that would take effect all over the South on January 1, 1863. But that would be like the U.S. government today trying to change the laws in Canada.

Alison: Right. We have no way of enforcing laws in Canada similar to the way Lincoln in the North had no way of enforcing a law in the rebel-controlled territories of the South in 1862.

Alison then goes on to explain to her students the purpose of this activity. She says that while she wants her students to understand the true circumstances surrounding the Emancipation Proclamation, she also wants them to see that textbooks are not perfect. She explains:

Textbooks and other types of nonfiction writing can sometimes be written unclearly or even be missing important information. Whenever you feel confused after reading something, ask yourself what the author is trying to say. It will enable you to see whether what you've read is written unclearly, is missing information, or is assuming you know something that you don't.

Why the Strategy Works (What the Research Says)

Too often in secondary classrooms, textbooks are upheld as ideal sources of information and learning. This is not surprising, considering the extent to which curricula are structured and revolve around textbooks. Without question, textbooks are valuable stores of information from which students can readily pull a wide variety of facts and ideas; however, they are not above criticism.

The Questioning the Author approach, developed by Beck, McKeown, Hamilton, and Kucan (1997), seeks to "depose the authority of the text" (p. 18). Beck and her colleagues noticed that many students who were having difficulties with texts that were unclear, poorly organized, or lacking essential information blamed their difficulties in understanding on their own inadequacies as readers. This, in turn, led to a reduction in students' self-confidence, eventually affecting the learning process across curricula and content areas.

Opening expository texts up to student interrogation encourages students to become involved in what they read. Questioning the Author instills in students the desire to actively construct meaning by interrogating the text. This approach, known as *constructivism*, is based on current research about how our brains and minds make meaning and has been explored by millions of teachers as well as noted researchers, such as Beck and Carpenter (1986), Brooks and Brooks (1999), Bruer (1993), and McGilly (1994).

To encourage active engagement with the text, Questioning the Author uses queries rather than literal questions. Queries are questions that ask students to look for gaps in their comprehension and see if those gaps are addressed by the text. For example, "What is the author trying to say here?" "Is there something the author is not telling us here?" "Do you think this would be more clear if . . . Why?" Queries perform three key functions:

- They guide students during initial reading and throughout the reading process.

- They create confident, constructive readers who are able to wrestle with challenging ideas within a text.

- They shift discussion from a student-teacher dynamic to a student-to-student forum in which authors' ideas are probed and evaluated.

Applications to Specific Content Areas

How Text Structures Differ From One Content Area to Another

With so much research pointing to the importance of being able to see the organizational patterns of texts (Derewianka, 1990; Dickson, 1995; Just & Carpenter, 1987; Pearson & Comperell, 1994), it seems appropriate to focus on the relationship between specific disciplines and the text structures commonly found in those disciplines' textbooks. We deal here with the disciplines of science, social studies, and math—the most textbook-driven subject areas.

In general, text structures stretch across several paragraphs of text, sometimes even whole sections of a chapter. The discipline that is the exception is math, where readings tend to come in smaller units and are commonly interrupted by problem sets or demonstrations. Because modeling and practicing using visual organizers has proven to be one of the most effective ways of teaching students how to see a text's structure, we have outlined the most common text structures in each subject area and provided useful organizers for each structure. To use them in the classroom and build student independence, follow the same steps as those provided for Text Structure and Visual Organizers, discussed earlier.

Common Text Structures in Science

The most common text structures in science textbooks are as follows:

Topic structures, or main idea structures explain a topic or central idea, the main subtopics, and key supporting details; see Figure 1.4.

Figure 1.4. Organizers for Topic or Main Idea Structures in Science Texts

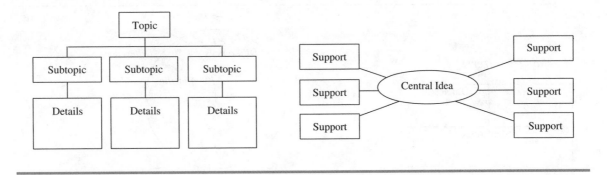

Figure 1.5. An Organizer for a Descriptive Structure in Science Texts

Useful Organizer:

Item	Criteria

Descriptive structures lay out a number of items and the criteria distinguishing each; see Figure 1.5.

Compare-and-contrast or classification structures explain two or more topics simultaneously, highlighting the similarities and differences between them; see Figure 1.6.

Generalization structures describe a general principle or idea (e.g., *a key idea in biological structure is that form fits function*) and the applications of that principle or idea; see Figure 1.7.

Problem-solution structures identify problems and describe their solutions, and *cause-effect structures* show the relationship between one set of events or ideas and another set of events or ideas; see Figure 1.8.

Process and cycle structures show the steps, phases, or events that make up a larger process; see Figure 1.9.

Figure 1.6. Organizers for Compare-and-Contrast and Classification Structures in Science Texts

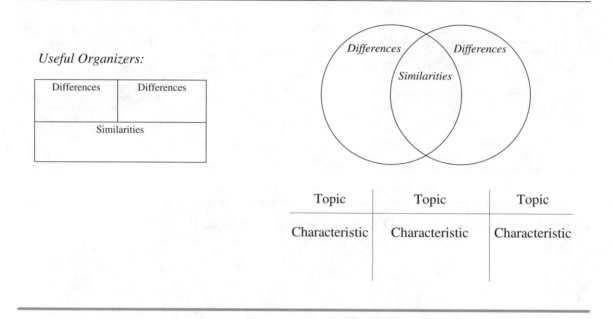

Figure 1.7. An Organizer for a Generalization Structure in Science Texts

Useful Organizer:

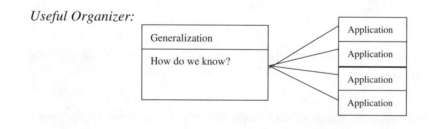

Figure 1.8. Organizers for Problem-Solution and Cause-Effect Structures in Science Texts

Useful Organizers:

Problem	Solution	Result

Cause	Effect

Figure 1.9. Organizers for Process and Cycle Structures in Science Texts

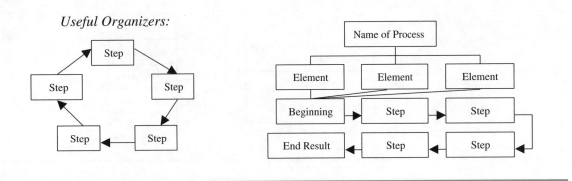

Figure 1.10. Organizers for Topic and Main Idea Structures in Social Studies Texts

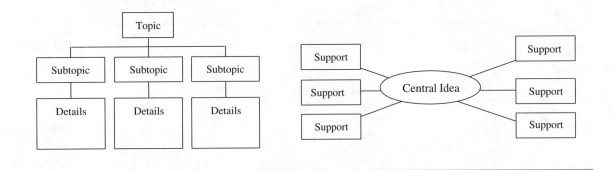

Common Text Structures in Social Studies

The most common text structures in social studies textbooks are the following:

Topic structures or main idea structures explain a topic or main idea, the main subtopics, and key supporting details; see Figure 1.10.

Generalization structures describe a general principle or idea (e.g., *the Nile River was central to Egyptian life*) and the applications of that principle or idea; see Figure 1.11.

Sequence structures present a set of related events in chronological order or show how specific events affect history; see Figure 1.12.

Figure 1.11. Organizer for Generalization Structures in Social Studies Texts

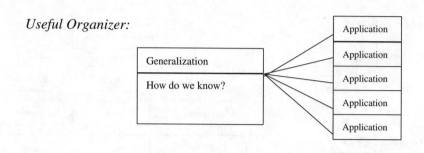

Figure 1.12. Organizers for Sequence Structures in Social Studies Texts

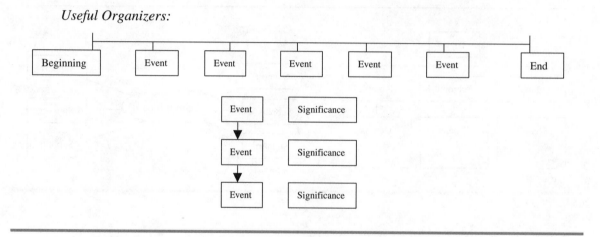

Compare-and-contrast structures set forth similarities and differences between two different items, events, or concepts; see Figure 1.13.

Problem-solution structures identify problems and describe their solutions, *cause-effect structures* show the relationship between one set of events or ideas and another set of events or ideas, and *question-answer structures* ask questions, answer them, and provide details; see Figure 1.14.

Common Text Structures in Math

The most common text structures in math are these:

Concept structures define key concepts and often include questions, formulas, or visual illustrations along the way; see Figure 1.15.

Figure 1.13. Organizers for Compare-and-Contrast Structures in Social Studies Texts

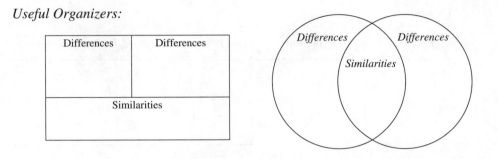

Useful Organizers:

Differences	Differences
Similarities	

Differences   *Differences*

Similarities

Figure 1.14. Organizers for Problem-Solution, Cause-Effect, and Question-Answer Structures in Social Studies Texts

Useful Organizers:

Problem	Solution	Result

Cause	Effect

Question	Answer	Details

Figure 1.15. Organizer for a Concept Structure in Math Texts

Useful Organizers:

Concept	Definition	Mathematical/Visual Illustration

Principle structures explain mathematical generalizations and often use mathematical formulas or visualizations to clarify the principle. Sometimes, real-world applications of the principle are described as well; see Figure 1.16.

Figure 1.16. Organizer for a Principle Structure in Math Texts

Useful Organizer:

Principle	Explanation	Mathematical/Visual Representation	Application

Figure 1.17. Word Problem Organizer for Math Texts

Useful Organizer:

What are the facts?	What steps will I take in solving it?
What is the question?	How can I represent the problem visually?
Solution	

Word problem structures ask students to read a problem, set it up in mathematical terms, and solve it; an example of a word problem organizer is shown in Figure 1.17. (See Note Making and Mathematical Problem Solving in Chapter 2 for a note-making system designed to help students solve word problems.)

Reading Charts, Maps, Graphs, and Tables in Science and Social Studies

Textbooks contain a lot of graphic material that can play a central or complementary role in textbook comprehension. Designed to help students better understand the prose they are reading, graphic material often has the opposite effect. Nevertheless, despite the importance of graphic material and the trouble it poses for students, instruction designed to process graphic material is rare (Fry, 1981).

One response to the issue of graphic material in textbooks is to use the *graphic information lesson* (Reinking, 1986). A graphic information lesson moves through three steps:

Step 1: Model with students the use and function of graphic material. Using a textbook, select a graph, table, chart, or map and explain to students how it works in relation to the text (is it central, supplemental, or redundant?). Ask students questions about the graphic material, including literal questions (e.g., How many settlers came to Jamestown in 1618? And how many were left in 1620?), interpretive questions (e.g., What does this astronomical death rate tell us?), and experience-based questions (e.g., Can you think of any other times when the death rate was disproportionately high? What can we learn from those situations?).

Step 2: Present simple graphics to students. Create simple graphic materials or find graphic materials from another text that relates to the textbook section. Ask students to decide whether these graphics are valid or invalid by using specific evidence from the text to justify their decision. Samples of these "homemade" graphics are shown in Figure 1.18.

Step 3: Ask students to synthesize their learning. After students have completed a lesson, they can apply their learning in one of two ways: They can create their own graphic material for the textbook section they have just read or they can evaluate how effectively the textbook's graphics were used.

Strategies for Struggling Readers

Research shows that students who struggle with textbook reading experience three distinct types of difficulty:

1. *Prereading problems*, such as activating prior knowledge and preparing for the reading

2. *During-reading problems*, such as reading actively and monitoring comprehension

3. *Postreading problems*, such as consolidating and elaborating on their understanding

Each of the strategies presented in this chapter (Visual Organizers, Peer Reading, Questioning the Author) relies on this before-during-after structure to maximize the potential for student success. However, sometimes, students will experience specific difficulties in one or more of these three areas. This section provides tips and reading strategies for addressing each area of difficulty separately.

Figure 1.18. Two Samples of Student-Made Graphics

Average Tobacco Exports From Virginia	
1613	200 lbs.
1616	2,500 lbs.
1617	8,839 lbs.
1618	49,518 lbs.

Letter From Third Governor

Sirs:

The colony is in great disarray. Only five or six houses are standing. The palisade (fence surrounding the town) has fallen down. The complete store of horses, goats, hens, sheep, and even cats and dogs has disappeared. The church is being used as a storehouse for produce, and every inch of town has been ploughed and planted, including the streets themselves.

Helping Students Overcome Prereading Problems

Provide cues or questions that help students develop a precomprehension grip on what they will be reading and that focus their attention on important information. Simple, single-sentence cues that provide important information and that help students develop a prereading image of the text are good ways to activate prior knowledge. For example, to help students conduct a reading of a textbook section on the development of our understanding of the solar system, a teacher could provide these cues:

■ This section is about scientists' attempts to understand planetary motion.

■ The scientists we will meet include Ptolemy, Copernicus, Galileo, Kepler, and Newton.

■ Thanks to scientists, we now know that the sun is the center of the solar system and that the planets revolve around it.

Similarly, you can provide prereading questions to direct students' attention to essential information:

- What are exponential functions?

- How do they differ from linear functions?

- How are exponential functions used in real life?

Ask students to form predictions before reading. Good readers intuitively make predictions about what a text will be about and then test their predictions against the text as they read. Struggling readers, on the other hand, often begin reading without forming any notion of what a text will be about. Remind students to form prereading predictions. To develop more powerful predictions, encourage them to scan the headings and pictures in the section or chapter, and make sure students understand that there are no wrong predictions. For even greater benefits, have students create prediction organizers to keep track of evidence in the text that supports or refutes their prediction (see Resource 1.9).

Use the Mind's Eye strategy to develop prereading visualizations. Visualization is a powerful entryway into a topic. By using the Mind's Eye strategy (Brownlie & Silver, 1995b, adapted from Escondido School District, 1979), you can help students build rich prereading images of a text's big ideas. Mind's Eye works like this:

Step 1: Select 20 to 30 key words from the text.

Step 2: Read the words slowly to students, one at a time and with feeling. Ask students to construct mental images as you read the words.

Step 3: Ask students to draw a picture, ask a question, make a prediction, or describe a feeling about the text based on the words. Allow students to show their products.

Step 4: Instruct students to read the text, comparing their initial ideas with what they discovered while reading.

Step 5: Encourage students to reflect on the process and the types of thinking they are most comfortable using (e.g., visualization, questioning, exploring feelings, predicting).

Distribute visual organizers in advance. When students see a visual organizer that maps out what they will be reading, it serves as a comprehensive preview of the text. Visual organizers reveal textual structure and help students to see how the big ideas fit together. (See the earlier discussion of Text Structure and Visual Organizers.)

Resource 1.9. Sample Prediction Organizer

My Prediction	Evidence For	Evidence Against	How My Understanding Has Changed

Helping Students Overcome During-Reading Problems

Model and allow students to practice using active reading processes. One of the most important factors in getting students to become active readers is teacher modeling. Show your students how you read a text. List the important steps on the board, and coach students through the process. Using a sample text placed on an overhead, conduct a Think Aloud session, in which you describe the thinking in your head out loud to students while you read actively. Give students practice time, feedback, and support as they practice the skills of active reading.

Using the foregoing suggestions for modeling and practice, directly teach struggling readers how to

- Mark essential information using a keyed set of symbols, such as these:

  * = This is important.

  + = This supports what I already knew.

  – = This contradicts what I thought I knew.

  ? = This is confusing; I have a question about this.

  ! = This is new information to me.

- Use visual organizers.

- Break a text into chunks and summarize each chunk before moving on.

- Make and monitor predictions.

Adjust levels of support. The basic structure of Peer Reading, in which students read sections of a text together and then stop to review it together, can be used at any time to accommodate struggling readers. What's more, the structure can be adapted to provide more or less support, depending on the student's needs. At a level of reduced support, both students might read the entire section, discuss it together, and summarize it. At a moderate level of support, both students might read the section in chunks and then one partner would coach the other partner through the process of summarizing the section; students then switch roles for the next chunk (summarizer becomes coach, coach becomes summarizer). At a high level of support, one student might read the section aloud to the other student before both students read it silently. After this double processing (listening to the text for the gist, reading the text for comprehension), students would serve as summarizers and coaches as usual. In all cases, encourage students to stop reading periodically to review, ask questions, make predictions, and assess their own understanding before going on.

Use cooperative structures. Help students manage during-reading difficulties by placing them in heterogeneous groups of four to six students. After modeling, allow students to practice and discuss active reading techniques, sharing their thoughts and ideas on what is difficult and what techniques work best to increase comprehension.

Use Questioning the Author. As described earlier, Questioning the Author is a group or whole-class strategy designed specifically around the constructivist principles of breaking the text into manageable chunks, reading actively by looking for gaps in comprehension, and holding collaborative discussions about the difficulties of textbook reading. Regular use of this strategy is a great way to assist struggling readers who feel that textbooks are lifeless, incomprehensible, or unmotivating.

Helping Students Overcome Postreading Problems

Use Peer Reading and Collaborative Summarizing. Both Peer Reading and Collaborative Summarizing (see earlier discussions) help students develop a systematic approach to consolidating comprehension into effective postreading summaries. For even better results, work with students to develop a set of criteria for developing and assessing summaries (e.g., Is it accurate? Is it clear and easy to understand? Does it include all the essential information and leave out all the trivial information?).

Give students the opportunity to demonstrate comprehension in multiple ways. Every classroom contains a variety of learning styles (see Chapter 7 for more on student styles). Just as students learn differently, they also demonstrate comprehension differently. After reading a text, some students may prefer to

- Restate the facts: What happened? Who was involved? Where did it occur? How did it occur?

- Make inferences and develop an interpretation: How would you explain _____ ? What evidence can you find?

- Develop images, hypotheses, or original products: What would happen if _____ ? Can you create a poem, icon, or skit to represent this?

- Explore values, personal feelings, and reactions: Why is _____ important to you? Can you describe your feelings?

Asking students to demonstrate understanding in a variety of ways allows them to work in their strongest styles, where they are most comfortable, and in the styles that need development.

Ask students to compare their prereading and postreading predictions. One of the best ways to engage postreading elaboration is to have students analyze how their prereading predictions were validated or disputed by the text. Using a prediction organizer, students not only collect evidence, they are also asked to explain how their understanding has changed as a result of reading (see Resource 1.9 again).

CHAPTER 2

Becoming a Thoughtful Note Maker

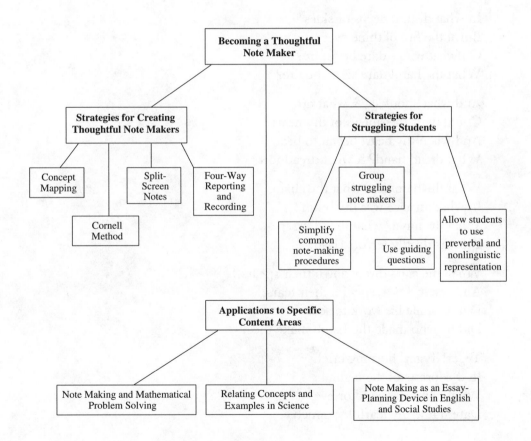

Note Making, Attention, and Comprehension: A Vital Connection

William Blake's famous poem "The Tyger" follows shortly. To Blake, the tiger is a symbol of awesome power, a symbol that mixes terror and majesty and that leads to bigger questions about its creator. Read the poem slowly, out loud to yourself. When you're ready, jot down some notes about the poem. Don't be afraid to write whatever comes to mind.

The Tyger

Tyger! Tyger! burning bright
In the forests of the night,
What immortal hand or eye
Could frame thy fearful symmetry?

In what distant deeps or skies
Burnt the fire of thine eyes?
On what wings dare he aspire?
What the hand dare seize the fire?

And what shoulder, & what art,
Could twist the sinews of thy heart?
And when thy heart began to beat,
What dread hand? & what dread feet?

What the hammer? what the chain,
In what furnace was thy brain?
What the anvil? what dread grasp
Dare its deadly terrors clasp?

When the stars threw down their spears,
And water'd heaven with their tears,
Did he smile his work to see?
Did he who made the Lamb make thee?

Tyger! Tyger! burning bright
In the forests of the night,
What immortal hand or eye
Dare frame thy fearful symmetry?

How do your notes reflect your thinking? Do you see in your notes specific tendencies, such as asking questions or developing associations? Perhaps, you were more inclined to focus on specific words, phrases, or images. Maybe you found yourself positively gushing with instant reaction. Notes are marks that represent our thoughts, nearly spontaneous eruptions of our minds as they struggle to make both sense and meaning of the words and ideas they encounter. To see

Figure 2.1. Student's Notes About "The Tyger"

I like the way it sounds—it has a nice flow, but I'm not sure I get it.
What are forests of the night? Sounds scary, like a horror movie.
He keeps asking questions.
He's asking about how the tiger got made—who made it? Is he talking
about God? Is God the "immortal hand"?
He's definitely afraid, because everything's described with words like
"dread" and "fearful" and "terrors."
The poet really makes you see the tiger in your head. I picture it lurking,
with its shoulder blades jutting up, ready to pounce.
In the beginning he says "Could frame thy fearful symmetry." But at the
end he says "Dare frame thy symmetry." I wonder if that's
significant.

---

this more vividly, look at Figure 2.1—the notes that a student from Georgia made about "The Tyger."

The student who created these notes was not interested in producing refined notes according to a particular note-making format. Rather, he was simply jotting down the ideas that came to his mind after and while he read "The Tyger." Yet even in this raw set of notes, we can see the ways in which this note maker engaged in specific types of thinking:

- He reacted personally to the poem (*I like the way it sounds*).

- He noticed that his comprehension needed to be improved (*I'm not sure I get it*).

- He used his own prior knowledge to develop a helpful association (*Sounds scary, like a horror movie*).

- He saw a pattern (*He keeps asking questions*).

- He found a central theme (*He's asking how the tiger got made*) and speculated on its meaning (*Is he talking about God?*).

- He determined the author's attitude (*He's definitely afraid*) and found evidence to support it (*Everything's described with words like "dread" and "fearful" and "terrors"*).

- He developed an image in his mind (*I picture it lurking*).

- He discovered an issue related to usage (*In the beginning, he says "Could frame . . ."*) and showed an eagerness to investigate further (*I wonder if that's significant*).

Figure 2.2. Colleen's Notes on Note Making

It's just the worst. In my American history class the teacher lectures at five hundred miles an hour. We all try to keep up, but it's no use. Five minutes into the lecture and my paper looks like a tornado hit it—dates, names, events, all of it crammed together, all of it virtually meaningless. I can hardly even use my notes to review for tests because they're such a mess. I wish [my teacher] would slow down a little and give us some time to catch up and also some time to think a little bit about what we're writing. Sometimes, I try to take notes when I read a chapter in my textbook, but sooner or later the same thing happens—there's just this mess of words on my page. There has to be a better way. I just wish someone would teach it to me.

What we see here is the power of note making. A few seemingly simple lines written in response to a poem prove to be quite deep, bristling with ideas, images, inquiries, and insights. Another way of saying this is that notes greatly increase both our attention and comprehension as readers by bringing out our minds' natural tendencies to focus their energies and search for the deeper meanings that animate texts. This link between note making, attention, and comprehension is well documented: In thirty-eight studies on the benefits of note making, thirty-five found that the act of recording ideas, of making notes, significantly increases students' attention and understanding of content (Kiewra, 1985).

Contrast this concentration of powerful thinking we find in one student's notes with the musings of another high school student named Colleen about note making (see Figure 2.2).

Colleen is certainly not alone among secondary students. Many middle school and high school students struggle when it comes to making notes, whether during lectures or while reading. In all probability, your own memories of college lecture halls and professional-development workshops dredge up unpleasant associations around the act of making and taking notes. Yet we know that notes, even in their rawest form, are powerful learning tools that focus attention and increase comprehension. So why such disparate images of notes?

Thoughtful Note Making:
The Difference Between Aha! and Blah

The truth is, with so many content standards facing teachers, the idea of teaching students how to become thoughtful note makers seems rather inconsequential to some. And so, content is covered at a blistering pace—lectures, textbook chapters, notes copied from overheads—while the student struggles to make sense of it all. This is Colleen's plight in a nutshell, and over time, it leads to a kind of numbness in students, the fatigue of being constantly overwhelmed. What students need is a set of structured note-making techniques that they can apply to different texts (and lectures). When various techniques are modeled, practiced, and discussed in the classroom, a new dynamic emerges, one that turns the numbness—the blah—into the aha! of focused understanding.

So, what is thoughtful note making? It is a process in which students learn to produce abbreviated versions of texts that highlight the central ideas and that make sense personally to the note maker. Thoughtful note making hinges on three central premises:

1. *Note making is an essential skill for academic success.* In high school, and even more in college, students must be able to make effective notes if they are to achieve success. Quite simply, without being able to produce a personal record of learning, it will be almost impossible for students to develop essential understandings or recall past learning in a meaningful way.

2. *Different texts and different individuals call for different techniques.* People are different, and texts are different. Thus it follows that notes can and should allow for variety as well. Students need to develop a repertoire of note-making techniques that they can use to make their reading meaningful.

3. *Note making needs to be taught directly, through modeling, practice, coaching, and discussions about application.* It is unreasonable to assume that students are hard-wired to make notes. Like any complex learning skill, note making needs to be taught. In the thoughtful note-making paradigm, this direct teaching is best accomplished through a three-step process:

1: *Model the note-making technique by thinking out loud.* The idea is to show students how you think your way through the process. For example,

> The first thing I do here is look for words and phrases that seem especially important and try to visualize them, actually see a picture in my head. When I see my picture, I sketch it in the left column. I make sure that my drawing represents the idea—I'm not trying to create a work of art here, just a sketch of what I see in my mind.

2: *Allow students to practice using the new technique by applying it to a particular reading.* While students are working, be an active observer: Coach students through the process and help them find ways to adjust the technique to meet their needs and preferences. For example,

> One of the hardest parts for me is staying focused on the big ideas and not drawing overly detailed pictures. So what I do is, I think

of icons, like No Smoking signs, and think about how they get all the important information into a simple sketch.

3: *Convene regularly with the entire class to talk about the problems students confronted and adjustments they made.*

In the section that follows, you will find four note-making techniques to model, practice, and discuss with your students:

- *Concept Mapping* is used to organize conceptual readings visually, according to the relationship between key ideas and supporting details.

- The *Cornell Method* harnesses the power of using questions to filter information and is ideal for reviewing learning.

- *Split-Screen Notes* help students visualize, to see the main ideas and important details, thereby aiding in their comprehension.

- *Four-Way Reporting and Recording* allows students to develop a repertoire of note-making strategies in order to select strategies that work best for them and to apply them to various texts.

Strategies for Creating Thoughtful Note Makers

Concept Mapping

Overview

This strategy helps students see how big ideas and supporting details form a relational structure. It also fosters critical thinking and stimulates spatial intelligence. The idea is simple: When students can "see" a concept and how its subtopics and details interrelate, higher-order thinking (e.g., writing about that concept, applying it, or connecting it to other learning and ideas) is greatly facilitated.

Steps in Implementation

1. Choose a topic, central question, or main idea from a reading for students to map. Model the process of mapping by showing students how subtopics and details radiate out from the central idea, topic, question, or concept.

2. Have students practice mapping out a reading. As they read and work, observe their note-making behavior and provide coaching.

3. Conduct a class review and discuss the process with students.

4. Encourage students to add to their maps, expose connections, or use their maps as study aids throughout the unit.

5. Allow students to practice mapping out readings on their own.

How the Strategy Works in the Classroom

Sarah Rosario wants her American History students to create a concept map of a reading on "The Branches of the U.S. Government." Although Concept Mapping is by no means a new note-making strategy, it is a favorite of Sarah's, for it gives her students a visually organized snapshot of a reading and provides for quick and easy reference later.

Sarah begins a modeling session where she will complete one branch of the organizer with help from the entire class:

Sarah: Topics and subtopics can be easy to identify in textbooks because they often stand out as headings and subheadings. For example, the heading of this chapter is? Gladys?

Gladys: Um. "Separation of Powers"?

Sarah: Exactly, so we put "Separation of Powers" in the center of our organizer. What's the first subheading you see? Jeremy?

Jeremy: "Executive Branch."

Sarah: So let's follow a branch off our central topic and write "Executive" in one of the outer circles. Now, let's read the paragraph and decide what details to put on the branches of the subtopic "Executive."

When Sarah has finished this branch, she has her students continue reading and filling in their organizers on their own while she circulates to see how students are faring and to provide coaching to students who are having difficulty. When everyone is finished, she conducts a review session on the board to make sure they have picked out all the important information and organized it properly (see Figure 2.3 for an example).

Why the Strategy Works (What the Research Says)

When students map a reading, they learn how to see the structural relationships between ideas, concepts, and details. By uncovering relationships in this way, mapping helps students bridge literal understanding to higher-order thinking and to tasks that involve application (Osman-Jouchoux, 1997). In addition, research conducted by Muth (1987) supports what teachers have been noticing for years: Students who know how to create maps that make the hierarchical pattern in texts explicit have a significantly easier time managing expository reading tasks (Resource 2.1 shows a blank concept map).

Figure 2.3. Concept Map, Student Example

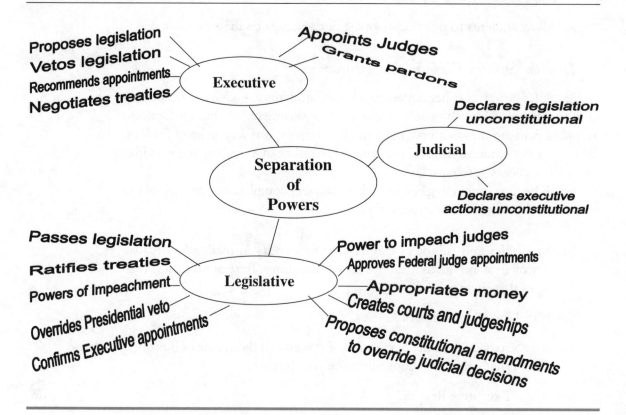

Cornell Method

Overview

Students use the Cornell Method (adapted from Pauk, 1974) to tease out main ideas and details from readings by asking summary questions about the text. Students can use these notes for reviewing and studying.

Steps in Implementation

1. Guide students in a survey of the text to identify topics and subtopics.

2. Have students convert the topics and subtopics into questions that will give shape to main ideas and probe for details.

3. As students read, have them stop periodically to fill in the details and main ideas as they emerge. You may want to model this process.

4. On completion of the reading, allow students time to review and refine their notes.

Resource 2.1. Concept Map

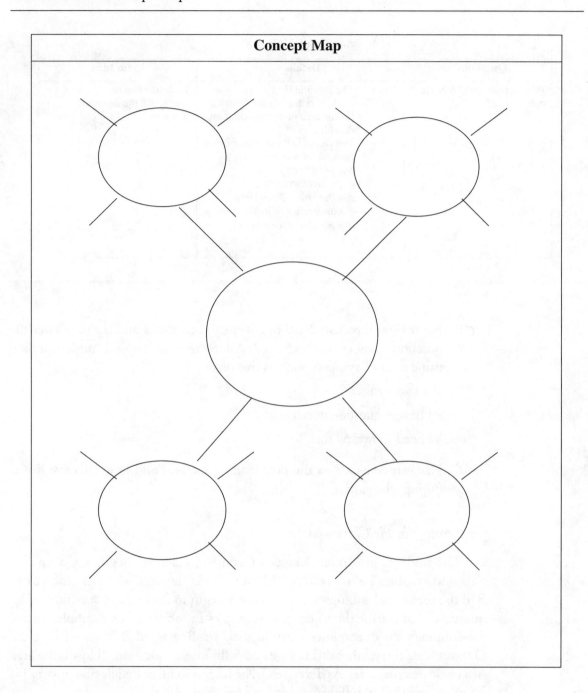

Concept Map

Figure 2.4. Area and Volume Graph

Area and Volume		
Questions	**Details**	**Main Idea**
How is the area of a circle determined?	• The formula for the area of a circle is related to the formula for the area of a parallelogram A = bh • The radius is the distance from the midpoint of the circle to any point on the circumference. • π is the ratio of a circle's circumference to its diameter. • π is equal to approximately 3.14…	To determine the area of a circle, use the equation $A = \pi r^2$

5. For review, direct students to cover up their notes and try to answer the questions they created in Step 2. Ask them to assess their understanding using a set of symbols such as this one:

   ✓ I know this.

   ? I have a question about this.

   * I need to review this.

6. Have students assess the note-making method and how effective it was during studying.

Strategy in the Classroom

The students in Miriam Kluger's Geometry class are beginning a unit on area and volume. Before reading, Miriam skims the text with her students to find the topics and subtopics. Her students begin to fill in their organizers with questions that mirror the topics and subtopics in the text. For example, one of the subtopics they encounter early in their reading is titled "Area of Circles." One student, Terry, takes this phrase and fashions the question, "How is the area of a circle determined?" As Terry reads, he begins to fill in details that answer his question and lead him toward a big idea (see Figure 2.4).

Terry continues filling in his organizer until he has extracted all the essential information from the reading. Later, when it comes time for him to study, Terry can simply refer to his organizer and test his knowledge by covering up the details and main idea columns to see if he can answer the questions. If he knows the answer to the question, he marks it with a "✓". If he has a question about it he marks it "?", and if he feels he needs more review, he puts a "*" next to the question.

Why the Strategy Works (What the Research Says)

A well-organized, clearly written text is obviously much easier for students to work with than one that is disorganized or unclear. Yet organization and clarity alone do not ensure student comprehension and retention of information. The Cornell Method (Pauk, 1974) provides a simple structure that allows students to build a brief synopsis of the main ideas and details in expository readings. By converting topics into questions, students learn how to filter essential information from a text: If information does not help to answer the question, then it is usually nonessential. An added benefit of the strategy is that it is a great study aid and makes it easy for students to determine the gaps in their comprehension. A blank, reproducible organizer for the Cornell Method is shown in Resource 2.2.

Split-Screen Notes

Overview

Many authors and texts rely on imagery to relate concepts, emotions, or ideas. Split-Screen Notes capitalize on students' spatial intelligence and enhance student memory by helping them to use visual representations, icons, and symbols to "see" big ideas and important details. Students then convert their visualizations into words, thereby doubling the power of their comprehension.

Steps in Implementation

1. Select a reading for students to read to themselves in class. It is generally a good idea to have students skim the passage to identify topics, subtopics, difficult vocabulary, and central themes.

2. Pass out Split-Screen Organizers (see Resource 2.3) and read the passage aloud while students draw pictures, icons, or symbols (not fine art!) to represent big ideas in the reading. Be sure to pause periodically to allow students ample time to draw.

3. Have students pair up to explain the images they created and to share big ideas and concepts they drew from the reading.

4. Direct students to use their images to create a product. (For example, if the reading is on the human vascular system, you might ask students to create a poster diagramming the flow of blood through vessels, veins, and organs. If the reading involves steps in a process, you may encourage students to create a comic strip outlining the steps.)

5. Encourage students to use Split-Screen Notes independently, as a tool for helping them to work through difficult reading passages visually.

Resource 2.2. Cornell Method Organizer

Cornell Method		
Questions	**Details**	**Main Idea**

Self-Assessment Key:

✓   I know this.
?   I have a question about this.
*   I need to review this more.

Resource 2.3. Organizer for Split-Screen Notes

Split-Screen Notes	
Image(s)	**Concepts, ideas, details explained**
Image(s)	**Concepts, ideas, details explained**
Image(s)	**Concepts, ideas, details explained**

Strategy in the Classroom

Students in Hallie Greenberg's English class have read Jonathan Edwards's famous sermon, *Sinners in the Hands of an Angry God*. But during class discussion, Hallie notices that many of her students are having trouble connecting the density of imagery to the overall meaning of the text.

Hallie decides to stop the discussion and asks her students to take out a piece of paper. She has each student fold a piece of paper in half lengthwise and says,

> I'm going to read an important excerpt from this sermon. What I want you to do is close your eyes and see in your mind what I'm reading. When particular images strike you as important, draw symbols or simple sketches of what you see.

Hallie then reads the excerpts slowly, with emotion and inflection. She pauses periodically to give students time to draw simple representations of images and ideas that stick in their minds.

When Hallie finishes reading, students pair off to explain their drawings and to use these drawings to identify the important ideas and details in the passage. As a synthesis activity, Hallie has students form groups of four to create a comic strip that uses both pictures and words to explain Jonathan Edwards's sermon.

Why the Strategy Works (What the Research Says)

Images are powerful tools for promoting understanding. For example, one of the key methods that enabled Albert Einstein to develop his groundbreaking theories was the creation of imaginary scenarios in his mind. Vladimir Nabokov, the famous Russian American author, would often have his students draw maps and pictures of scenes and images in the novels they studied to deepen their understanding of the text.

As readers, if students cannot make effective images—if they cannot imagine what Coketown looks like in *Hard Times,* or visualize how white blood cells attack foreign agents, or see the conditions inside a slave ship on the Middle Passage, or create a visual representation of a word problem in math—then they are missing essential information. The importance of image making to the reading process is corroborated by many researchers, including Keene and Zimmerman (1997), Pressley (1977), and Sadoski (1985).

Split-Screen Notes (adapted from Siegel, 1984, and Brownlie, Close, & Wingren, 1990) takes advantage of students' natural inclination to create images while reading; moreover, it helps them refine the skill so that it is focused on summarizing essential information. Working in conjunction with this non-linguistic processing is the linguistic filtering of information as students discuss their images and convert them into the key ideas and details they contain.

Figure 2.5. Phase 1: Adaptation Note-Making Sheet

Phase 1: Review	
What is an adaptation?	**Reptile adaptations**
How do species adapt?	**What happens to a species that can't adapt?**

Four-Way Reporting and Recording

Overview

Because students learn and process information in different ways, a single note-making technique will not serve the needs of all learners. Four-Way Recording and Reporting allows students to develop a repertoire of note-making strategies so that they are able to select strategies best suited both to their own styles and to particular texts.

Steps in Implementation

Four-Way Reporting and Recording involves five phases:

Phase 1: Review. Before beginning Four-Way Reporting and Recording, it is a good idea to conduct a whole-class review of the different methods of recording ideas on paper (e.g., Concept Mapping, Split-Screen Notes, outlining, Cornell Method, simple listing). After the review session, students break up into groups of four, and each group member becomes responsible for a different reading related to a larger topic. For instance, if the topic is animal adaptation, the four subtopic readings might be, "What is an adaptation?" "How do species adapt?" "What happens to species that can't adapt?" "Reptile adaptations." Students divide their paper into four quadrants and label each quadrant according to the title of the text each student is reading (see Figure 2.5).

Phase 2: Reading. Students read their text, select a method of note making, and record the key ideas and supporting details from their text in the quadrant pertaining to their subtopic.

Figure 2.6. Phase 3: Partners

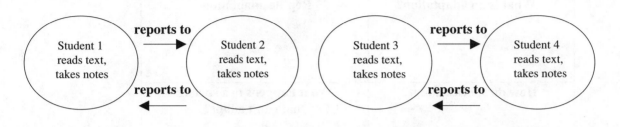

Phase 3: Partners

Phase 3: Partners. Students pair up. Partners use the notes they created in Phase 2 to report key ideas and supporting details from their respective readings. While each partner reports on his or her reading, the other takes notes using a different note-making technique than the one used in Phase 2 (see Figure 2.6).

Phase 4: Group Reporting and Recording. In this phase, each student reports to the whole group on what was presented to him by his partner. During this presentation, the student who originally researched this topic checks his or her partner's presentation for accuracy. The remaining group members take notes in the appropriate quadrant. Once again, students must use a note-making tool that they have not used previously. This process repeats until all four quadrants have been completed by all four students (see Figure 2.7).

Phase 5: Synthesis and Reflection. After all the students have reported and recorded, they work either individually or cooperatively on a synthesis task that draws on all four readings. For example, Stephan Maby uses Four-Way Reporting and Recording in his language arts class by having students report and record on four great speeches: The Gettysburg Address and excerpts from famous speeches by Martin Luther King Jr., John F. Kennedy, and Franklin Roosevelt. Afterward, students use their notes to develop a list of criteria for great speeches. Time is also provided for students to reflect on the process and to discuss how they might better use it next time.

Strategy in the Classroom

Barbara Roth is conducting a lesson on adaptation with her tenth-grade biology class. Over the past month, she has been focusing on different note-making strategies, including Concept Mapping, Power Notes (a variation of outlining), simple listing, and the Cornell Method. Now, she wants students to begin developing independence in learning how to decide when to use each strategy.

To begin, she breaks her students into groups of four and provides each member of each group with a separate reading from their textbooks on adapta-

Figure 2.7. Phase 4: Group Reporting and Recording

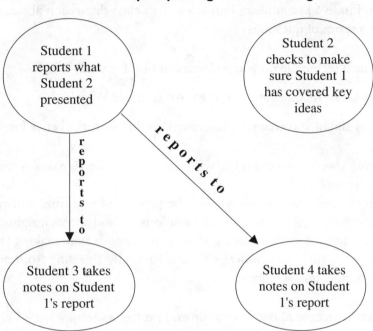

Phase 4: Group Reporting and Recording

tion. Along with the reading, Barbara distributes a Four-Way Reporting and Recording Organizer (see the end of this section for a reproducible blank form).

"Today, we're going to begin the lifelong process of learning how and when to use notes to help us as readers," she tells students; then she goes on to explain how Four-Way Reporting and Recording works and what students do during each of its phases. While students work, Barbara monitors their progress and provides coaching and assistance on how to select particular strategies and how to use them well while reading.

After students have completed their readings on adaptation independently and taken notes using their preferred technique in Quadrant 1 of their organizers, they pair up to begin Phase 3.

John and Myra have formed a pair. Using his notes, John reports to Myra what he learned from his reading titled "What is an adaptation?" As he reports, Myra takes notes in the "What is an adaptation" quadrant of her organizer using a new note-making technique. Afterward, John and Myra switch roles. Myra reports to John from her reading on reptile adaptation while John takes notes, this time using a simplified outlining procedure called Power Notes.

In Phase 4, pairs come together to report and record again in groups of four. Using his notes again, John reports the key points from Myra's reptile adaptation reading to Susan and Patrick. As he speaks, Susan and Patrick take notes in the "Reptile adaptations" quadrant of their organizers. During John's report, Myra listens and checks to make sure John is accurately reporting what she told him. Students rotate through this process in their groups until everyone has reported once, checked once, and recorded twice so that each student uses four different note-making techniques. John's completed organizer is shown in Figure 2.8.

When Phase 4 is complete, Barbara sparks class discussion about the strategy using a series of questions:

- Which technique do you feel worked best for you? Why?

- Which technique gave you the most trouble? Why?

- How might you change this strategy so that it works better for you?

Students share their thoughts with the class while Barbara records their responses on the board.

When all students have completed the process of reporting and recording using four different techniques, the class reflects on and shares insights, sources of difficulty, and the value of being able to use various note-making strategies. Barbara has her students synthesize their learning by choosing from one of the following culminating activities:

1. Create a simile about adaptation and explain it. Adaptation is like _____.

2. Make a diagram showing how different animals are specially adapted to their environments. Present your diagram to the class.

3. Write an essay describing how adaptation is an essential component of Darwin's theory of Evolution.

Why the Strategy Works (What the Research Says)

Rather than providing students with another way of recording information, Four-Way Recording and Reporting (Brownlie & Silver, 1995a) instead asks students to synthesize their knowledge of note-making procedures by selecting and applying a variety of techniques from their toolbox. This note-making tool works off all four forms of communication as students are required to read, listen, speak, and write while engaging in sophisticated cooperative behaviors. Because it is a synthesizing technique, it assumes students have developed competency in a variety of note-making tools. For these reasons, Four-Way Reporting and Recording is ideally suited for practicing and for helping students see how the different tools in their burgeoning note-making repertoire can be applied in a variety of situations—to different kinds of texts, to reading versus listening, to research, and as foundations for oral and written presentations and projects.

The goal of the strategy is to help students find and develop four or five note-making strategies that work best for them. This way, students become comfortable, competent, yet flexible note makers. In addition to the note-making tools described in this chapter, other ways for students to record information

Figure 2.8. John's Organizer on Adaptation

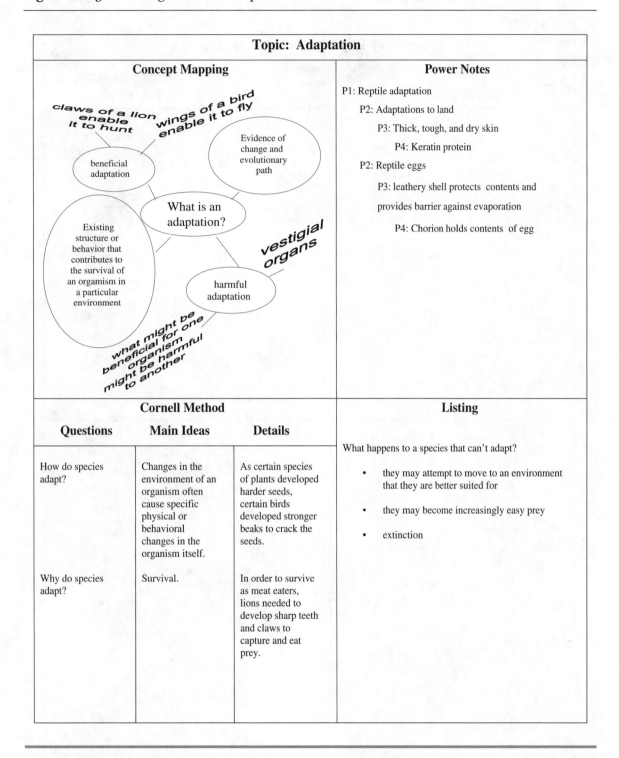

include key words, pictures, lists, graphic organizers, diagrams, charts or graphs, linking ideas (e.g., using lines, color coding, etc.), flow charts, time lines, signs or symbols, and outlines. See Resource 2.4 for the blank, reproducible organizer for Four-Way Reporting and Recording.

Resource 2.4. Four-Way Reporting and Recording Organizer

Four-Way Reporting and Recording
Topic: _____

_____	_____
_____	_____

Applications to Specific Content Areas

Note Making and Mathematical Problem Solving

Mathematical word problems are often frustrating for students and teachers because they combine reading and math skills. Frequently, students try to jump to a solution rather than focusing on what they are being asked to do. Math Notes (adapted from Thomas, 1999) teaches students how to use a note-making technique to examine the components of word problems and to think through the problem-solving process. The technique is based on what Sternberg (1999) identifies as the five essential components of mathematical reasoning:

1. The ability to identify a problem

2. The ability to mentally represent the problem

3. The ability to formulate problem-solving strategies

4. The ability to allocate time effectively by engaging in presolution thinking

5. The ability to evaluate one's own work

Math Notes works like this:

Step 1: Model the process of solving word problems using a blank Math Notes organizer. Modeling the process means teaching students how to solve word problems by

- Identifying facts and missing information

- Determining the central question, exposing hidden questions, and discarding irrelevant information

- Developing a visual representation of the problem

- Listing the steps in solving the problem

- Solving the problem

Step 2: Teach students how to check their work. Thorough evaluation of one's own work means checking for *accuracy* (were mathematical operations done correctly?), *reasonableness* (does the answer make sense?), and *appropriateness* (does the solution answer the question?).

Step 3: Allow students to practice using the technique, and encourage them to keep a notebook. As students practice using Math Notes and apply the technique on their own, they should keep a notebook of all the problems they've solved using Math Notes. This notebook should become a yearlong reference for students to use in identifying different types of patterns and for finding effective problem-solving

Figure 2.9. Example of Math Notes Technique

At 11:00 pm, a jet leaves Cheyenne for Pittsburgh traveling at 600 mph. One hour later, at midnight, a different jet leaves Pittsburgh for Cheyenne, traveling at 700 mph. The distance between Pittsburgh and Cheyenne is 1427 miles. The jet to Pittsburgh travels at an elevation of 5000 feet. The jet to Cheyenne travels at an elevation of 6000 feet. Find the time when the two jets will pass each other.

Facts	**Steps**
What are the facts? • Jet 1 leaves at 11:00 pm; Jet 2 leaves at midnight. • Jets travel toward one another. • Distance from Cheyenne to Pittsburgh is 1427 miles. • Jet 1 travels at 5000 ft, Jet 2 travels at 6000 ft. *What's missing?* • Distance jets will travel when they meet. • Equation: d = rt.	1. Set up equation: $600t + 700(t-1) = 1427$ 2. Solve equation: $1300t - 700 = 1427$ $t = 2127/1300$ $t = 1.64$ hours 3. Convert time into standard form: $1.64 = 1$ hour, 38 minutes 4. Answer the question: Planes will pass each other at 12:38 am.
Questions	**Visualization**
What's the problem asking? At what time will two planes meet? *What are the hidden questions?* If $d1 = rt$ and $d2 = st$, when will $d1 + d2 = 1427$ miles? *What is irrelevant?* How high the jets travel is irrelevant information.	11:00 pm Cheyenne 1427 miles 600 mph 700 mph midnight Pittsburgh

---

models that have worked for them before. See Figure 2.9 for an example of this technique.

Relating Concepts and Examples in Science

Of all the disciplines, science is the one most dense with concepts. A simple survey of a biology, earth science, physics, or chemistry textbook will reveal a

Figure 2.10. "Structure of Matter" Concepts

shape	reactive	neutron	reactant
density	non-reactive	isotope	transfer of energy
flexibility	metals	states of matter	radiation
texture	gases	solid	heavy elements
toughness	mass	liquid	half-life
color	nucleus	gas	unstable
reaction	electron	ion	stable
atoms	proton	nuclear reaction	

Figure 2.11. Concept Examples

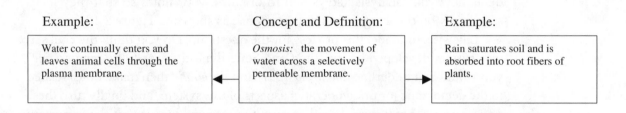

Example:

> Water continually enters and leaves animal cells through the plasma membrane.

Concept and Definition:

> *Osmosis:* the movement of water across a selectively permeable membrane.

Example:

> Rain saturates soil and is absorbed into root fibers of plants.

web of interrelated concepts. For example, a chapter in a chemistry textbook titled "The Structure of Matter" might contain all of the concepts shown in Figure 2.10.

One of the most powerful ways of making abstract examples understandable to students is the inclusion of examples. Yet even when clear examples are provided, many students have trouble connecting them to the abstract concepts they illustrate. This simple note-making technique makes seeing and remembering crucial concept-example relationships easier for students (see Figure 2.11).

Note Making as an Essay-Planning Device in English and Social Studies

Writing a thoughtful essay in English or Social Studies means more than getting the sequence of ideas right. In fact, one of the major impediments to generating high-quality written responses to essay questions on tests is thinking too early about the sequence and format of the writing. Before students can consider the question of textual arrangement, they must first be able to analyze the question and establish categories in notes that will enable them to get their thinking into the open.

For example, to model this process with a question that asks students to discuss the difference in Robert Frost's use of imagery in "Desert Places" and "Stopping by the Woods on a Snowy Evening," you would underline the words

Figure 2.12. Imagery–"Desert Places," "Stopping by the Woods"

Imagery in "Desert Places"	Imagery in "Stopping by the Woods"

difference, imagery, and the titles of the two poems. Then, you would show the students how your analysis allows you to organize your notes so that they focus specifically on the imagery in the two poems, as shown in Figure 2.12.

Likewise, to model this process for the question, "Do you think the civil service system developed by the Tang and Song dynasties was fully democratic?" you would first underline *civil service system* and *democratic*, then make notes related to the democratic (or undemocratic) aspects of this system, and finally turn these notes into a concept map. In either case, the essential idea is that the important information is generated *before* the student begins worrying about the format and sequence of the essay. When notes contain the information that is responsive to the question, organization for the essay is greatly facilitated.

Strategies for Struggling Note Makers

The importance of modeling, practicing, coaching, and whole-class discussions about the application of various techniques cannot be overstated when it comes to developing students' note-making skills. For those students who continue to experience difficulty, try these suggestions:

Simplify common note-making procedures. Do not let a procedure get in the way of a student's ability to apply a technique. If, for example, a student is having trouble remembering the correct lettering and numbering format for building an outline, try using Power Notes (Sparks, 1982). In using Power Notes, students build a traditional outline, but they use only the numbers 1 through 4: 1s represent main ideas; 2s to 4s represent increasing levels of specificity. For example,

Topic: Polygons

1. Triangles
  2. Three sides
    3. scalene
      4. no equal sides

        3. isosceles
            4. two equal sides
        3. equilateral
            4. three equal sides
1. Quadrilaterals
    2. Four sides
        3. square
            4. four equal sides
        3. rhombus . . .

This way, the confusion caused by having to remember outlining, capitalization rules, when to use Roman versus Arabic numerals, and so on, is alleviated.

Group together struggling note makers. When struggling note makers work in cooperative groups while taking notes, they have the opportunity to talk about what works and what causes them confusion. In addition, group note-making sessions help students to see what key information they missed while taking notes and to pay better attention to their note-making behaviors.

Use guiding questions. When students produce notes that contain too much detail or that lack focus, guiding questions provided before reading will help them assume control over the note-making process. Guiding questions can be text-specific (e.g., "What are the properties of light? What evidence suggests light is made of particles? What evidence suggests light is a wave?") or they can be general questions that students can apply to any reading. For example, when students encounter readings that explain concepts, they may use any of these questions to develop a comprehensive set of notes:

- What is the concept?

- What does it look like?

- What are its parts?

- What is its purpose?

- How does it work?

- How did it originate?

- What is it part of?

- What is its importance?

Allow students to use preverbal and nonlinguistic representation. Readers create images spontaneously while reading, and research shows that this skill helps proficient readers develop high levels of comprehension, which struggling readers often fail to reach (Keene & Zimmerman, 1997). Help struggling note makers build this critical skill by using Split-Screen Notes and Image Making, both described earlier.

CHAPTER

3

Managing and Mastering Vocabulary

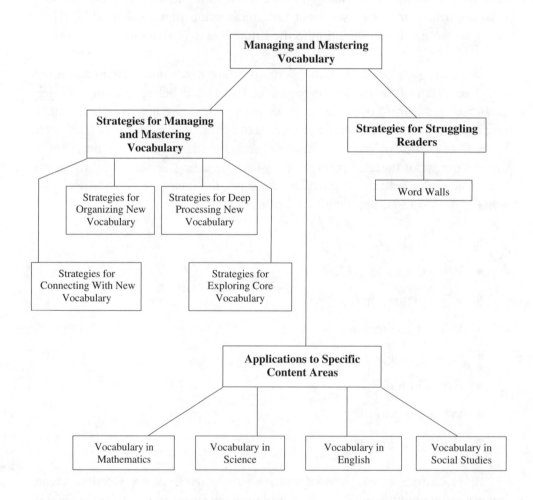

Managing and Mastering
Vocabulary

Strategies for Managing
and Mastering
Vocabulary

Strategies for Struggling
Readers

Strategies for
Organizing New
Vocabulary

Strategies for Deep
Processing New
Vocabulary

Word Walls

Strategies for
Connecting With New
Vocabulary

Strategies for
Exploring Core
Vocabulary

Applications to Specific
Content Areas

Vocabulary in
Mathematics

Vocabulary in
Science

Vocabulary in
English

Vocabulary in
Social Studies

62

CHAPTER

3

Managing and Mastering Vocabulary

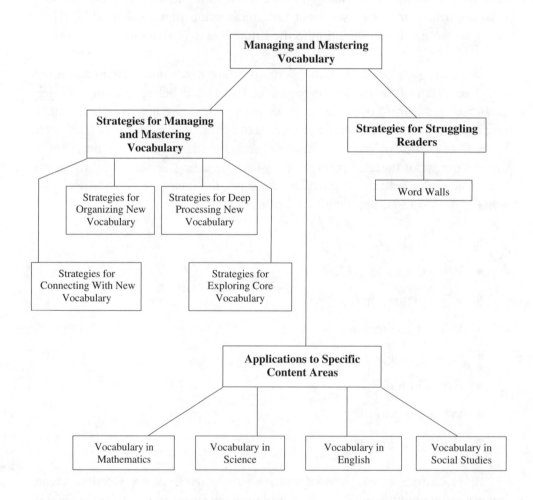

62

Both common sense and more than five decades of research tell us that vocabulary is essential for students to understand what they read. Without an understanding of new and important words, and without solid strategies for processing and remembering the new vocabulary they encounter when they read, students will struggle. The first step, however, in helping students to process, remember, and understand new words is to see that there is more than one kind of vocabulary. To get a sense of this, read the three passages that follow. The first is a snippet from a poem by the great African American poet Langston Hughes, the second is taken from a World History textbook, and the third is a math problem.

1. Droning a drowsy syncopated tune,
   Rocking back and forth to a mellow croon,
   I heard a Negro play.

2. Although it proved a major controversy for the church in the 1200s, Saint Thomas Aquinas's scholasticism would be a significant step toward the explosion of knowledge that would come to define the Renaissance.

3. Create a function that accurately represents the rate of acceleration shown by the data.

Students across the country labor through passages like these on a daily basis, and the main reason for their struggle can be summed up in two words: unfamiliar vocabulary.

In passage #1, for example, the average high school student may have trouble with the words *syncopated* and *croon*. Lacking an understanding of these words, a student may still be able to piece together the image of a musician playing a tune while rocking back and forth to a mellow something, but he'd have trouble imagining what kind of tune and why, exactly, the man is rocking back and forth. What the student misses without these kinds of words are the details that bring imagery into focus and the finer layers of meaning that lend richness and beauty to poetry and prose.

Words like *scholasticism* in passage #2 represent an even greater threat to student comprehension when not properly explored. How could a student unfamiliar with scholasticism appreciate the connection between Thomas Aquinas and the birth of the Renaissance? Would the student understand how rational thought made its way back into mainstream thinking after hundreds of years? Probably not. Without important words like these, students are hindered in their ability to make thoughtful generalizations.

Last, imagine the sheer terror and confusion of the student, encountering the problem in passage #3 in the middle of a unit on functions and their graphs, who still doesn't have a firm grasp of what a function is! Not understanding core content words, such as *function,* can doom a student to struggle for weeks or even a whole year, attempting futilely to build understandings on a weak foundation.

Figure 3.1. Vocabulary Importance Chart

Type of word	Level 1 core content	Level 2 important	Level 3 nice to know
What the word does	Concepts or ideas that lay the foundation for entire units of study or disciplines.	Concepts, events, people, or places that deepen understanding and facilitate connections between content.	Nouns, verbs, adjectives, adverbs, specialized vocabulary, etc., that enrich language but are not central to understanding.
Suggested time spent mastering words	Anywhere from one week to several months, depending on the centrality and importance of the concept.	From fifteen minutes to a couple of class periods, depending on importance.	From one to ten minutes, depending on student comprehension speed.

In the foregoing three passages, it is easy to discern a certain hierarchy of vocabulary, not unlike the hierarchy Wiggins and McTighe (1998) outline in their model for "establishing curricular priorities." Wiggins and McTighe seek clear distinctions between indispensable knowledge and that which is simply nice to know. In the classroom, where content is considerable yet time is limited, such distinctions are essential. By applying this evaluative method to vocabulary instruction, we get a useful filter for determining the importance of different vocabulary and how much time might be spent on each type (see Figure 3.1).

Once you determine the importance of a word, you can use vocabulary strategies to help students connect with, organize, deeply process, and explore unfamiliar words. To help us remember the four critical steps in making vocabulary memorable, we use the acronym CODE.

In this chapter, you will find strategies and tools to help your students

- _C_onnect with new vocabulary.

  Students remember information when it is strongly connected to what they already know or have experienced.

- _O_rganize vocabulary.

  Students remember information when it is clearly organized, especially when they are faced with many new or unfamiliar words.

- *D*eep process vocabulary.

  Students remember and understand information best when it is processed using visual, auditory, physical, or emotional experiences and then practiced frequently.

- *E*xplore core vocabulary.

  Students internalize and build new understandings when they are given the opportunity to think about, examine, and reexamine concepts in a variety of ways.

Strategies for Connecting With New Vocabulary

Because so many words that students encounter in secondary classrooms are new and unfamiliar, students need as many "handles" as possible to give them a precomprehension grip on new terms and concepts. These tools help students connect with new vocabulary by activating their prior knowledge and by helping build an increasing sense of comfort and familiarity with new vocabulary.

Building Associations

Even when new words are entirely unfamiliar to students, you can still tap into their prior knowledge by using open-ended, associative prompts like the following:

Have you ever heard of the word *ecosystem?*

What words do you see in *ecosystem?*

What do you associate with *ecosystem?*

You can then help students shape their precomprehension associations into preliminary definitions. For instance, if a student sees the word *system* in *ecosystem* and associates *eco* with ecology, then a good preliminary definition might be *an ecological system.*

Generating Preliminary Definitions

When students have to generate preliminary definitions for new words, it forces them to survey their prior knowledge; look for meaningful prefixes, suffixes, and root words; analyze the context of the reading for clues; and generate any associations they can. Then, by asking students to compare their own definitions with those in a dictionary or glossary as well as with the way the word is being used in the text, you promote analysis and deep engagement with the word, leading to improved understanding and recall.

Figure 3.2. Excerpt From a Chemistry Vocabulary Journal

Desalinate

I know that the prefix de- can mean "to remove from." I also remember that the suffix -ate can mean "having" or "acting upon." I'm not sure what -salin- is, but the reading is about seawater which is salty and -salin- looks similar to salt. So I think "desalinate" means to remove the salt from something that has salt.
   {Dictionary def: desalinate.
   {(verb) desalt; to remove the salt from.
It looks like I was dead-on.
A good sentence for this word would be:
The survivors had to *desalinate* the ocean water before they could drink it.

As an example, Figure 3.2 shows an excerpt from a student's vocabulary journal in chemistry.

Auditory Exercises

Even though most teachers would dismiss a foreign language teacher who gave students new vocabulary but never asked students to say these words aloud, many content area teachers do exactly the same thing. Regularly saying words and their definitions aloud and with emotion and writing them out as a class or individually breeds comfort, familiarity, and recall.

Strategies for Organizing New Vocabulary

Organization: Most of us wish we had more of it in our daily lives. When we organize clothes, tools in the garage, address books, notes—and, of course, vocabulary—we are helping our often-unreliable memories to remember. When organized, specific items are easy to identify, quickly recalled, and more likely to be remembered over longer periods of time.

Students who have no system of organizing new vocabulary find it difficult to manage and remember many individual bits of information. The tools and strategies in this section teach students how to use grouping and mapping to systematize the vocabulary they encounter.

Vocabulary Organization

Because a typical unit has so many new words and phrases, it is important to organize words around core concepts. When words are categorized by common threads and linked to the overarching structure of a unit, students see how the

Figure 3.3. Vocabulary Organization for an Ecology Unit

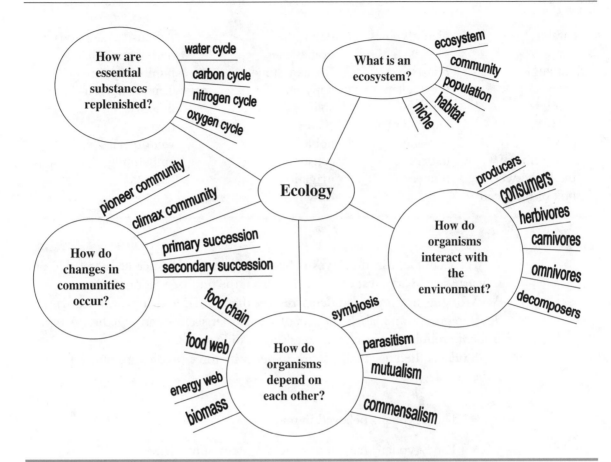

terms fit together to form a big picture. In addition, by slotting specific vocabulary words into a comprehensive framework, the problem of information overload is greatly reduced.

In Figure 3.3 is a biology teacher's organization of vocabulary for a unit on ecology. Notice how she converted each core concept into an essential question and then connected new vocabulary to each question using a concept map.

Inductive Learning

A constructivist twist on vocabulary organization asks students to organize words into meaningful categories on their own or in groups. This classification technique, based on a learning model developed by Hilda Taba (1971), helps students construct a personally resonant image of a unit's structure and make predictions about content based on key vocabulary. (Vocabulary words need to be a mix of familiar and unfamiliar words so students can create categories using their prior knowledge.)

Figure 3.4. Key Words From a Unit on Ancient Egypt

pharaoh	hieroglyphics	delta	Amon-Ra (sun god)
vizir	scribes	granaries	herbal remedies
right angle	priests	Rosetta Stone	number system
survey	polytheism	papyrus	Temple at Abu-Simbel
pyramids	surgery	sphinx	dynasty
Nile River	inclined plane	slaves	basing
Shadoof	bureaucracy	nobles	wet/dry seasons
Osiris (God of	traders	censer	embalming
the Underworld)	farmers	irrigation	grain tax
Book of the Dead		Edwin Smith papyrus	

For example, Martin Reyes is beginning a unit on Ancient Egypt. He presents students with a list of key words from the unit (see Figure 3.4).

Working in groups, students review the words, look up new words, and develop groups and labels for sets of words that seem to go together. A typical student grouping looks like the one shown in Figure 3.5.

Students then use their groups to generate three predictions about the text. For example,

- The Egyptians believed in many gods.

- The Egyptians had an advanced system of medicine.

- The Egyptians used math to solve everyday problems.

As students read, they collect evidence that supports or refutes their predictions.

Strategies for Deep Processing of New Vocabulary

The processes of storing vocabulary in long-term memory and quickly retrieving words and their definitions are closely related. The latter is refined through practice, whereas the former is attained through deep and active thought. For the most part, vocabulary strategies that are familiar to most of us have focused on retrieval, using rote memory techniques, such as writing out definitions, finding synonyms and antonyms, using flash cards, or solving analogies. Although these strategies can be helpful, research (Marzano et al., 1988) shows that well-constructed memory strategies engage deeper thinking processes. In other words, students must be encouraged to actively process vocabulary and to

Figure 3.5. Student Grouping—Ancient Egypt

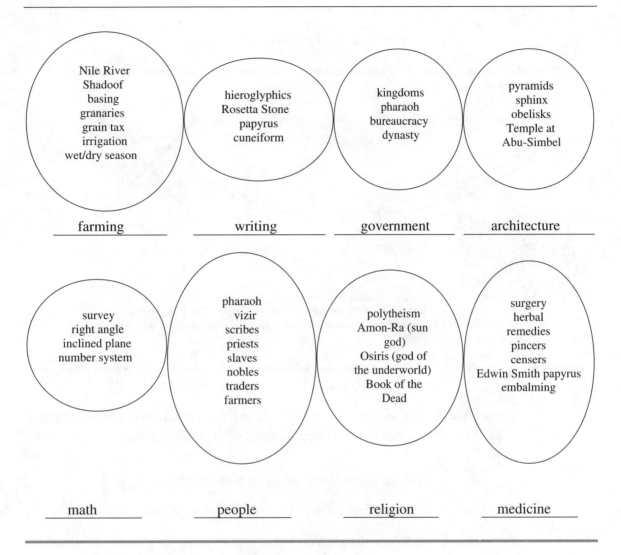

examine it from multiple angles to strengthen their understanding of it, thus making retrieval easier and practicing more productive.

The strategies and tools in this section are designed to combine the fundamentals of deep and active thought with practice techniques to help students master vocabulary.

Visualizing Vocabulary

Research shows that when knowledge is *dual coded*, constructed and stored both through language and through nonlinguistic representation, it becomes more meaningful and easier to recall (Paivio, 1990). The strategy called Visual-

Figure 3.6. Post-Reformation Europe–Vocabulary

Post-Reformation Europe —Vocabulary

Absolutism: form of government where monarchs have complete, or absolute, political power over their subjects.

I drew a crown because power in absolutism is held by a king or queen. The sword with the people represent the absolute power of the monarchy over the people. The voting box with an X through it reminds me that this form of government is the opposite of democracy, where the people have the power.

izing Vocabulary uses pictures and words to enhance students' understanding of key vocabulary terms. Visualizing Vocabulary works like this:

Step 1: Students define the word using a dictionary or glossary.

Step 2: Students draw three or four pictures that represent the word.

Step 3: Students write a sentence that explains why the pictures are good representations of the word.

In the example shown in Figure 3.6, we see the work of a ninth-grade World History student who used Visualizing Vocabulary to help him deeply process the word *absolutism*.

Intensifying Vocabulary

Dual coding (Paivio, 1990) is the process of making learning deeper and more memorable by processing information through words as well as through other, nonlinguistic means. Intensifying Vocabulary is a tool that maximizes the power of dual coding by asking students to process and retrieve new vocabulary in four distinct ways:

Figure 3.7. Intensifying Vocabulary

Kinesthetic Understanding	Emotional Understanding
Make a physical symbol with your body or hands that explains what *probability* means to you.	What are or might be some of the feelings you associate with the idea of *probability*? Describe your feelings.
Linguistic Understanding	**Visual Understanding**
In your own words, write down what *probability* means to you.	Create a picture in your mind of *probability*. What does probability look like?

1. By explaining the term in words (linguistic understanding)

2. By representing it visually (visual understanding)

3. By linking it to emotional responses (emotional understanding)

4. By representing it physically (kinesthetic understanding)

Figure 3.7 shows an example.

Multiple Intelligences Processing

Much like Intensifying Vocabulary, which is based on the fact that multiple methods of storing information improve recall, Multiple Intelligences Processing gives students eight distinct ways to process and store vocabulary words and their definitions. The tool is based on Howard Gardner's (1983, 1999) influential theory of multiple intelligences, which redefined our notion of what it means to be smart by breaking intelligence down into eight distinct intelligences. Thus, Multiple Intelligences Processing means using as many intelligences as needed to store information deeply. See Figure 3.8 for examples.

Peer Practice

Research studies on cooperative learning have proven the benefit of allowing students to work together to complete structured tasks (Johnson, Maruyama, Johnson, Nelson, & Skon, 1981; Walberg, 1999). The strategy called Peer Practice is a review and practice technique that can maximize the learning and retention of new vocabulary by pairing students up into player-coach relationships so

Figure 3.8. Multiple Intelligences Processing

To store information through ...	A student would ...
Verbal-linguistic intelligence	Say/write the word and one's own definition.
Logical-mathematical intelligence	Compare the word to another word.
Spatial intelligence	Visualize the word and its definition.
Bodily-kinesthetic intelligence	Make a physical gesture using the hands or body that represents the word.
Musical intelligence	Associate the word with a song/sound, or sing the word and its definition.
Interpersonal intelligence	Study the words with a partner; quiz and coach one another.
Intrapersonal intelligence	Determine what the word means at a personal level, or how it is relevant to one's own life.
Naturalist intelligence	Study the words outside, or develop nature-based associations for each word.

that each student receives the benefits of each role. The strategy moves through four steps:

Step 1: Break students up into pairs. Explain to students that they will be acting as both a player, answering questions on selected vocabulary and listening to the coach's feedback, and a coach, checking the player's answers, encouraging the player, and helping the player through difficulty.

Step 2: Provide Peer Coaching sheets to each player and each coach (see Figure 3.9 for sample Peer Coaching Sheets).

Step 3: Instruct each Player A to begin answering the provided questions. Instruct each coach to provide praise, encouragement, and help (but not the answer!) when Player A gets stuck. Circulate around the room to monitor player-coach interaction.

Step 4: Have students reverse roles. Player A becomes the coach, while the coach becomes Player B. Over time, encourage students to use the player-coach structure of Peer Coaching on their own as review and practice strategies for vocabulary internalization.

Figure 3.9. Sample Peer Coaching Sheet

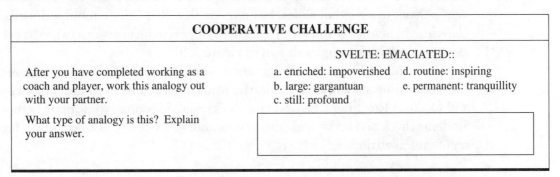

Player A Questions	Coach B Answers
Directions: Circle the featured pair that best expresses the relationship similar to that expressed in the original pair and explain why.	**Directions:** Use these answers and clues to guide your partner's thinking.
1. TRANQUILITY: PEACE:: a. chaos: disorder b. retraction: indictment c. combustion: waste d. miracle: relief e. tension: relaxation	1. A sundial is a <u>tool</u> for measuring time and a balance is a <u>tool</u> for measuring weight. Also, both sundial and balance are ancient measuring devices. A thermometer measures temperature, which may be related to illness but doesn't measure illness.
2. GROTESQUE: DISTORTED:: a. fabricated: efficient b. monotonous: constant c. trustworthy: optimistic d. imagined: permanent e. mature: young	2. Lack of identity is the <u>defining characteristic</u> of something that is anonymous; lack of form is the defining characteristic of something that is amorphous. Pairs c and d fit the pattern of "defining characteristic" but not the pattern of "lack of."

Player B Questions	Coach A Answers
1. SUNDIAL: TIME:: a. balance: weight b. pyramid: worship c. umpire: score d. thermometer: illness e. metronome: music	1. Peace is a defining characteristic of tranquillity and disorder is a <u>defining characteristic</u> of chaos.
2. ANONYMOUS: IDENTITY:: a. amorphous: form b. masked: party c. wealthy: income d. motivated: goal e. infamous: report	2. Distortion is a <u>defining characteristic</u> of grotesque and constancy is a <u>defining characteristic</u> of monotony.

COOPERATIVE CHALLENGE	
After you have completed working as a coach and player, work this analogy out with your partner. What type of analogy is this? Explain your answer.	SVELTE: EMACIATED:: a. enriched: impoverished d. routine: inspiring b. large: gargantuan e. permanent: tranquillity c. still: profound

For example, Radu Petra uses Peer Coaching to help students practice for the analogy section of the SAT. He provides each player-coach pair with a set of worksheets. Notice how the answers to Player A's questions are on Player B's sheet and vice versa. This is because while A is answering each question, B is coaching A (and vice versa). (See Figure 3.9 for excerpts from Radu's worksheets.)

Strategies for Exploring Core Vocabulary

The most important vocabulary words need to be explored deeply by students. When students have the opportunity to focus their attention on core vocabulary, to examine, refine, and revise their understanding of central ideas and concepts, they are able to develop powerful generalizations and navigate more easily through the discipline.

The strategies in this section are designed to turn vocabulary instruction into the kinds of quests for meaning that drive learning in any discipline.

Concept Attainment

The meaning of a word is more than just a simple dictionary definition. This is especially true for concept words, such as *evolution* in science, *function* in math, or *capitalism* in history, where a deep understanding of single words is crucial to constructing future understanding. One of the best ways to help students build a meaningful base of crucial concepts is to use the Concept Attainment strategy.

As a vocabulary strategy, Concept Attainment works like this:

Step 1: Ask students to generate their initial associations of a word or concept. For example, Carly McLaughlin, a language arts teacher, asked her students to generate their preliminary ideas for the concept *tragic hero*.

Step 2: Provide students with examples, which contain all the critical attributes of the concept, and nonexamples, which contain some—but not all—of the critical attributes. Ask students to determine what all the examples have in common and how the examples differ from the nonexamples. Encourage students to discuss and refine their ideas. For example, to help her students begin to discover the critical attributes of a tragic hero (e.g., is a prominent person, has good qualities, has a tragic flaw that brings about a downfall, gains insight before death), Carly asks her students to form groups to analyze the examples and nonexamples shown in Figure 3.10.

Carly then asks students to generate a preliminary definition of *tragic hero*. After discussing student definitions, she reads descriptions of Michael Corleone and Oedipus Rex (tragic heroes) and Rocky and Superman (not tragic heroes). Students check and revise their definitions and, as a whole class, generate a final set of critical attributes.

Step 3: Ask students to apply their understanding. To help her students synthesize their learning, Carly asks them to create their own tragic hero and to describe him or her in one paragraph. Students must make sure they have included all the critical attributes in their description.

Figure 3.10. Concept Attainment–Tragic Hero

Case 1: Hamlet, Prince of Denmark (yes)
The hero of this famous Shakespearean play is a sensitive and subtle thinker, but his ability to see all sides of an issue makes it almost impossible for him to take decisive action. When his father's ghost appears and demands that he be avenged, Hamlet's inability to act stirs up a host of resentments and plots against him. Near the end, Hamlet discovers the value of action and dies heroically, finally avenging his father and cleansing Denmark of evil.

Case 2: Macbeth, the Thane of Cawdor (yes)
Macbeth is a great soldier and a brave man, but the central figure of the Shakespearean play is also a secretly ambitious man. When the king visits the castle, Macbeth kills the king and takes control of the country. Macbeth's violent attempts to conceal his guilt and consolidate his power provoke more and more opposition. In the end these forces overwhelm him. Before his death, however, Macbeth attains new insight into himself and dies bravely, his former nobility and courage restored.

Case 3: Ronald Reagan (no)
A sports reporter from a small midwestern town, Ronald Reagan became a Hollywood screen actor achieving wealth and fame. He was elected head of the Screen Actors' Guild and became an effective politician and great communicator. He ran for president of the United States and won. His unprecedented move from actor to president of the United States caused many to consider him one of the most effective politicians of the last half century.

Case 4: Frank Yanko (no)
Frank Yanko represents what is best about the United States. Frank sells used cars in southern New Hampshire. He is successful, makes a fair amount of money, and seems happy much of the time. He is a good father and a supportive, faithful husband. Frank gets along well with his neighbors, is a member of two civic groups, and attends church regularly. He goes out of his way to be helpful to his older, less able neighbors.

SOURCE: Adapted with permission from Silver, Strong, & Perini (in press).

Vocabulary Notebook

The Vocabulary Notebook strategy (adapted from Silver et al., 2001) combines elements of other vocabulary tools to form a comprehensive system for managing and exploring the important concepts in a text or texts. The strategy builds reading independence, and its notebook structure helps students keep a yearlong track of their vocabulary development. The strategy also facilitates review. Vocabulary Notebook moves through four steps:

Step 1: Students read through a selected text and mark each difficult word using the following symbols:

✓ = I know this word

___ = I think I know this word (underline word)

⬭ = I don't know this word (circle word)

Note: You may need to provide students with photocopies to facilitate text marking.

Step 2: For each difficult word, students write their own definition. Students should use context clues, prefixes, suffixes, and root words to help formulate preliminary definitions.

Step 3: Students look up words in the dictionary, decide which meaning is being used in the text, and record the appropriate definition. Students then compare their own definitions with the actual definitions by identifying similarities and differences.

Step 4: Students select the one to three word(s) they believe are most important to the text and complete a set of processing activities for each selected word (classification, analogy, visual representation, and synonyms).

For example, Anna Jurkiewicz is having her American History students read Martin Luther King Jr.'s "Letter From A Birmingham Jail." Figure 3.11 shows a selection of words from a student's Vocabulary Notebook for the reading.

From these and other words, the student chose *unjust* as the most important word and completed the processing activities described in Figure 3.12.

Applications to Specific Content Areas

Vocabulary in Mathematics

Much of the mathematics that students learn in middle and high school is presented to them as pieces of knowledge in the form of axioms, postulates, theorems, and the like. For example, it is not uncommon for students in their first year of Algebra to encounter the following axiom: The graph of $y = ax^2 + bx + c$ is a parabola. Students are expected to memorize and apply this kind of information, but problems arise when students have not mastered the larger concepts (e.g., quadratic equation, linear equation, etc.) that give context and clarity to

Figure 3.11. Vocabulary Notebook—"Letter From A Birmingham Jail"

Word	My Definition	Dictionary Definition	Comparison
legitimate	allowed	Sanctioned by law or custom; lawful; conforming to or abiding by the law.	The sense of my definition was right, but not specific enough. The dictionary definition makes it clear that something legitimate is recognized by the law.
segregation	A time when African Americans used to have separate schools.	The policy or practice of forcing racial groups to live apart from each other.	I thought of segregation more as a time period, but the dictionary calls it a practice or policy.
unjust	unfair	Unfair; contrary to justice.	I was right on this one. Unjust and unfair are synonyms.

SOURCE: Adapted with permission from Silver et al. (2001).

such statements. In fact, much of the vocabulary in mathematics is composed of broad concepts with specific, identifiable attributes. For this reason, math vocabulary, which contains a multitude of core content words, readily lends itself to Concept Attainment (see earlier discussion), where students take sufficient time to identify and process the critical attributes of core concepts.

To keep these concepts close at hand and fresh in students' minds, the use of vocabulary journals can also be very effective. When organized as a kind of glossary, students' journals should contain the following:

- Clear explanations of concepts, followed by appropriate examples that elucidate the concept and show practical applications

- A list of the different kinds of problems students can expect to encounter, followed by ways to identify them and the concepts they pertain to

Vocabulary in Science

In science, the sheer volume and the highly specialized nature of most scientific words is daunting to most students. These difficulties can be managed by encouraging students to get into the following three habits:

Figure 3.12. *Unjust* Organizer

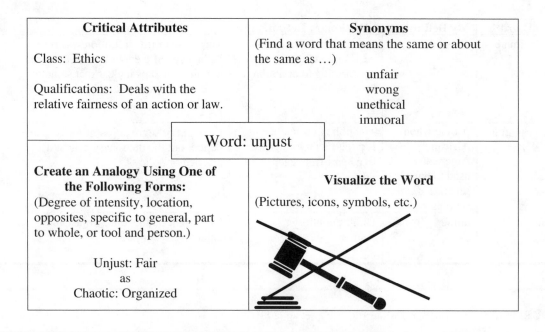

Critical Attributes	**Synonyms**
Class: Ethics	(Find a word that means the same or about the same as ...)
Qualifications: Deals with the relative fairness of an action or law.	unfair wrong unethical immoral

Word: unjust

Create an Analogy Using One of the Following Forms:	**Visualize the Word**
(Degree of intensity, location, opposites, specific to general, part to whole, or tool and person.)	(Pictures, icons, symbols, etc.)
Unjust: Fair as Chaotic: Organized	

1. Organize the new vocabulary they encounter. Because science is not unlike a foreign language in terms of the number of words students are asked to memorize and understand, it is essential that students have strategies for organizing unfamiliar words. Inductive Learning and Vocabulary Organization (see Strategies for Organizing New Vocabulary) are excellent strategies for helping students manage large numbers of words.

2. Practice unfamiliar vocabulary frequently. Research shows that, on average, students must encounter unfamiliar vocabulary at least six times before they are able to understand and internalize its meaning (Jenkins, Stein, & Wysocki, 1984). To this end, strategies like Visualizing Vocabulary, Multiple Intelligences Processing, and Peer Practice (see Strategies for Deep Processing of New Vocabulary) as well as more traditional techniques, such as memory cards, student-created glossaries, and drill and practice provide effective ways for developing the level of familiarity suggested by the research.

3. Connect to new vocabulary by activating prior knowledge. Scientific words are often completely unfamiliar to students. Connecting such words to what students already know by generating preliminary definitions; examining prefixes, suffixes, and root words; building associations; or simply saying and repeating the word out loud (see Strategies for Connecting With New Vocabulary) can give students the confidence they need to manage and internalize science vocabulary.

Vocabulary in English

Aside from grammatical vocabulary (e.g., *pronoun, dependent clause, gerund*) and the academic vocabulary of literary analysis (e.g*., metaphor, foreshadowing, tone, symbolism*), most of the vocabulary students encounter in English has to do with the richness of authors' language–the words writers use to create vivid images, develop characters, build suspense, and so forth. A common problem students face when dealing with this kind of vocabulary lies in the way meanings shift and vary, depending on their context. In fact, in some cases, a student's prior knowledge can actually get in the way of understanding what an author means when he or she chooses certain words. This can be true at a technical level (e.g., when a student understands the word "compass" to mean a device that determines direction rather than an instrument for drawing circles, the interpretation of John Donne's poem "A Valediction: Forbidding Mourning" will be off base). It can also be true at an interpretive level (e.g., if a student defines a common word like *insanity* too narrowly, he or she may have a hard time when authors like J. D. Salinger, Shakespeare, or Charlotte Perkins Gilman challenge the meaning of the word). The importance of context in English means that students need to be able to determine how what they already know is connected to what's written in the text. Strategies such as Generating Preliminary Definitions and Vocabulary Notebook are helpful here, provided there is a strong emphasis on how the words are being used by the author.

Vocabulary in Social Studies

In mathematics, we saw that students encounter difficulty when they don't understand the broad concepts behind specific declarative statements. Social Studies produces a similar sort of problem. Social Studies textbooks are filled with generalizations like this: "In all civilizations, environment affected the adaptation and evolution of cultural tools." The problem is that these generalizations attempt to impart knowledge using concepts such as *civilization, environment, adaptation, evolution, culture,* and so on, that students haven't completely internalized. Because so many of the generalizations and statements in Social Studies readings use certain words and concepts repeatedly, it can often be very helpful to turn these words into Essential Questions (see Chapter Five). For example, using questions such as "What makes a culture a civilization?" or "How did early American colonists adapt to their new environment?" can help students explore core concepts and use those concepts to drive their reading.

Strategies for Struggling Readers

Many struggling readers are sensory learners, for whom vocabulary is often too abstract. Traditional direct vocabulary instruction championed by some researchers (see Stahl & Fairbanks, 1986) lacks the kind of multisensory approach to learning vocabulary that many struggling readers respond to. Encouraging nonlinguistic representations of words, processing words using all eight intelligences, and using frequent independent and group practice to help students internalize words and their meanings are all aspects of Intensifying Vocabulary that can help turn struggling readers into proficient readers. In addition, vocabulary games that borrow the structures of popular games, such as Outburst® and Pictionary®, and multimodal review sessions, such as acting out words, choral review, and repeating words and definitions with emphasized emotion also facilitate storage and recall.

Frequent practice with and exposure to unfamiliar words cannot be stressed enough with respect to students who have trouble with vocabulary. One way to increase student familiarity with new words is to use the Word Wall strategy. Word Wall works like this:

Step 1: Students read a text, either for homework or class work, and identify any words that are new or unfamiliar to them.

Step 2: When they finish reading, students come together as a class to share some of the words they identified as new or unfamiliar. The teacher records these words on a poster or the chalkboard.

Step 3: The class defines each word the teacher records and then generates one, two, or three synonyms for each word, which the teacher also records on the poster or chalkboard (generating the Word Wall).

Step 4: Individually, students work through a synthesis activity by writing a summary of, personal response to, or a thesis essay about the text they read. Students must use between five and ten of the words from the Word Wall correctly in their writing.

To maximize student practice with new words, the Word Wall can remain displayed for an entire unit. Each time students engage in a writing task, they should draw on words from the Word Wall to master the unit vocabulary and to enrich and enliven their writing.

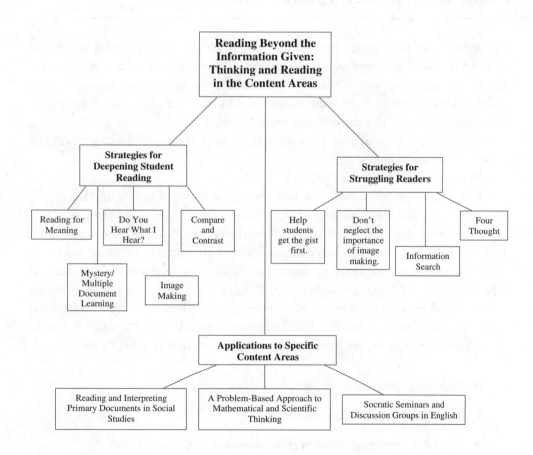

CHAPTER

Reading Beyond the Information Given

4

Thinking and Reading in the Content Areas

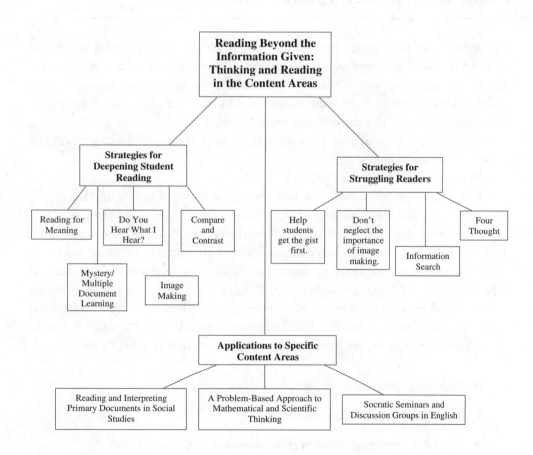

81

Figure 4.1. Image of Standardized Test

Which of the following ingredients is not necessary for photosynthesis to take place in plants?

a) sunlight
b) nitrogen
c) carbon dioxide
d) water
e) chlorophyll

This Is Not Your Grandfather's Standardized Test

For more than fifty years, the words *standardized test* have called a particular image into the minds of American students and teachers: number two pencils, grainy scratch paper, tiny white circles awaiting gray fillings, and questions that, although tricky, focused too often on bits of information rather than deep understanding—questions like the one shown in Figure 4.1.

Now, take a look at four test items from new state tests from around the country, shown in Figure 4.2.

Hmmm. Something has changed.

It is interesting to examine the way these new kinds of test items change the definition of what it means to read well. On earlier standardized tests, students were primarily asked to recall small (often trivial) pieces of information from a text; on today's standards-based exams, students are asked to systematically separate the important information from the trivial or inconsequential. As little as five years ago, reading items appeared only on reading tests. Now they make up a substantial portion of items in *all* content areas. When we took standardized tests, the most frequent reading items measured our ability to identify the main idea in a passage. Now, our students are taking tests that require them to

■ Interpret complex maps, graphs, tables, and charts

■ Draw and support conclusions

■ Establish meaningful connections between multiple texts

■ Collect, organize, and critique evidence used to establish a claim or support a hypothesis

In general, we might say that the tests of an earlier generation focused primarily on the information in the text; today's tests ask students (in Jerome Bruner's

Figure 4.2. A Test Sampler

A Test Sampler
(Selected items from new state tests)
1999-2001

Science

Students are given a collection of tables displaying data relating the consumption of alcohol to birth defects. They are asked to examine the data and write a brief essay exploring the viability of the hypothesis that consumption of alcohol causes birth defects. In their essay they are challenged to offer a critique on the data and suggest what other data should be collected to strengthen the hypothesis.

Social Studies

Students are provided with eight documents describing the purpose of government from a variety of cultures and periods of history and asked to write an essay in which they discuss how the concept of political authority changes over time in different cultures. Average length of document: 75 words.

Math

Students are given a mathematical formula $c = 3t/4 + t^2$ and a graph displaying changes in the concentration of medication over time. They are asked to draw conclusions and support them with evidence about the effects of changes in the timing of different dosages over time.

English

Students read a short story, a poem, and an excerpt from a memoir. All three pieces deal with relationships between adolescents and senior citizens. On the basis of these readings they are asked to compare and contrast the ways in which the different pieces deal with the intergenerational theme that unites them.

[1957] insightful phrase) to "go beyond the information given." In other words, these tests ask students to think as well as they read. Now we have to ask ourselves, do we have the strategies that will help students learn the following?

- The content they are expected to learn

- The skills they need to comprehend the texts they are given

- How to combine thinking with reading to go beyond the information given

The answer is "yes."

In this chapter, we will explore five research-based strategies for developing the skills of deep reading:

1. *Reading for Meaning* focuses on finding, evaluating, and marshaling textual evidence.

2. *Mystery or Multiple-Document Learning* helps students read a set of texts that may include both visual and printed material and extract and develop a central theme.

3. *Do You Hear What I Hear?* builds skills in listening, reading, speaking, and writing so that students can interpret even the most challenging texts.

4. *Image Making* underscores the importance of creating mental visualizations while reading in order to build a deep, lively, and multidimensional understanding of a reading.

5. *Compare and Contrast* teaches students how to read two or more texts comparatively and determine the critical similarities and differences between them.

After describing the strategies, we will focus on some of the key content-specific issues, including deep reading in the various disciplines, and we will outline effective techniques for assisting struggling readers.

Strategies for Deepening Student Reading

Reading for Meaning

Overview

Reading for Meaning is a strategy that helps students develop informed, well-supported interpretations of the texts they read. Difficulties students encounter while reading come in four distinct types: (a) difficulties with the literal meaning; (b) difficulties in seeing important ideas or central themes; (c) difficulties with ambiguous, symbolic, or image-laden language; and (d) difficulties with personally or emotionally challenging texts. This strategy addresses these difficulties through focused statements that help students filter and process the text, find and evaluate evidence, and build a thoughtful interpretation.

Steps in Implementation

1. Create three to six statements keyed to important information in the text. Statements can focus on literal information (e.g., Lincoln believes the Gettysburg soldiers have died in vain), on inference of central ideas and themes (e.g., Lincoln sees a linear relationship between past and present), on connections and contexts outside the text (e.g., a good slogan for the Gettysburg Address would be "We can work it out"), and on emotional content and personal meaning (e.g., Lincoln wants to make Americans feel guilty about the war).

2. Review the purpose and goals of the strategy with students, and introduce them to the topic and text.

3. Explain the use of the Reading for Meaning organizer, and have students make initial predictions about the reading by deciding if they agree or disagree with each statement.

4. Ask students to read the passage carefully and collect evidence to support and refute the statements on the organizer.

5. Direct students to form small groups to discuss the statements and share responses and thoughts on the reading.

6. Engage students in a whole-class discussion on the content and the process, and ask them to apply what they've learned to a writing task or project.

Strategy in the Classroom

As part of a three-week unit on Intolerance and Tragedy in American History, Joseph Kim's students are studying the plight of Indian nations during U.S. expansion. Joseph will have his students examine the poignant primary document *Memorial of the Cherokee Nation, 1830,* in which the Cherokee people of Georgia respond to their forced relocation. During a previous lesson on slavery, Joseph noticed that his students were having difficulty using evidence from their texts to develop informed interpretations of the events. In response, he has chosen to conduct a Reading for Meaning lesson.

Before reading, Joseph provides his students with an organizer containing six statements that ask students to make predictions about the reading. His students review the statements and make prereading predictions by deciding whether they agree or disagree with each statement. After they have made their predictions, Joseph's students begin to read the *Memorial*. Joseph reminds them to read carefully to be sure that they are citing the proper evidence to either support or refute their initial predictions. For example, one student's organizer is shown in Figure 4.3.

After students have completed their reading and cited evidence to support or refute the six statements on their organizers, they gather in small groups of three or four to discuss the statements and share some of the evidence they collected during reading.

When his students have had ample time to share information within their groups, Joseph calls the whole class together for a discussion. Together, they discuss passages that shed light on the central issues of relocation and the perspective of the Cherokee people.

To synthesize their learning, Joseph's students begin an examination of the account their textbook gives of the Native American relocation. Their task is to determine whether the textbook tells the whole story of Native American relocation or whether it is a partial or biased account. Once students have collected ideas and organized their thoughts, Joseph has them compose a formal letter to the editors of the textbook noting recommended improvements for the text.

Figure 4.3. Sample Student Organizer

☐ agree ☑ disagree	**1. The authors of this piece believe in the laws of the United States.**	
	Support	**Refute**
		"It is incredible that Georgia should ever have enacted the oppressive laws to which reference is here made...."
☐ agree ☑ disagree	**2. For Cherokees, moving west of the Mississippi is preferable to being oppressed in their homeland.**	
	Support	**Refute**
		"We wish to remain in the land of our fathers." "If we are compelled to leave our country, we see nothing but ruin before us."
☐ agree ☑ disagree	**3. All people have the same rights under the Constitution.**	
	Support	**Refute**
		The Constitution guarantees liberty and the right to our property, but the Cherokees had their freedom and property (or land) taken from them.
☑ agree ☐ disagree	**4. The authors are afraid that even if they move, the U.S. government will force them to relocate again in the future.**	
	Support	**Refute**
	The Indians in that territory "will regard us as intruders." "We see nothing but ruin before us."	
☑ agree ☐ disagree	**5. Relocation is an inhumane policy.**	
	Support	**Refute**
	Cherokees would come into conflict with other tribes west of the Mississippi. The region was badly supplied with food and water, and they were forced to go against their will.	
☑ agree ☐ disagree	**6. History has shown that all of the Cherokees' fears were justified.**	
	Support	**Refute**
	They were forced to relocate by way of what was called the Trail of Tears. Many Cherokees died. There are very few Cherokees alive today.	

Why the Strategy Works (What the Research Says)

Consider the following statement made by a teacher at a workshop on improving student reading:

> I don't understand why my students aren't more engaged when they read. I go out of my way to make sure the material is interesting. We practice reading constantly in class, but whenever I read [my students'] papers, I can see that they are having trouble finding main ideas and supporting their own ideas with evidence from the text.

Statements such as this one are often heard, and they stem from a common misconception that making meaning is as simple as reading words on a page.

Research, however, has shown that reading should be approached strategically, that the act of constructing meaning from texts is a multifaceted process involving prereading, during-reading, and postreading stages. Researcher Beth Ann Herrman (1992), for example, sees strategic reading and writing as a "complex thinking process used before, during, and after reading and writing to construct meaningful interpretations" of texts (p. 428).

Taking cues from this three-phase approach and adapting a model from Harold Herber's (1970) work with Reading and Reasoning Guides, Silver et al. (1996) designed the Reading for Meaning strategy to help students read actively and critically:

- During prereading, students examine statements about the reading and decide whether they agree or disagree. The goal here is to form an intuitive idea of the text's structure and to activate students' prior knowledge, which they can use to connect with the text.

- During the active-reading stage, students are driven by a purpose. They naturally slow down their reading and search more deeply for evidence that will either support or refute their prereading predictions.

- Postreading takes shape when students are asked to reflect on the evidence they have collected and how their understanding of the content has changed or evolved as a result of the reading. Often, a synthesis task helps students to apply their learning to a meaningful context.

Resource 4.1 is a reproducible organizer for the Reading for Meaning strategy.

Resource 4.1. Reading for Meaning Organizer

	1.		
		Support	Refute
☐ agree ☐ disagree			
	2.		
		Support	Refute
☐ agree ☐ disagree			
	3.		
		Support	Refute
☐ agree ☐ disagree			
	4.		
		Support	Refute
☐ agree ☐ disagree			
	5.		
		Support	Refute
☐ agree ☐ disagree			
	6.		
		Support	Refute
☐ agree ☐ disagree			

Mystery or Multiple-Document Learning

Overview

When a five-year-old asks why the sky is blue or a cosmologist ponders the origins of the universe, they are gripped by the wonder of a mystery. The Mystery Strategy captures students' interest by posing a mystery to be solved, a problem to be worked out, or a situation to be explained. In solving the mystery, students learn to

- Gather, organize, and process information from a variety of clues

- Formulate and test hypotheses

- Think creatively and analytically to solve problems

- Develop, defend, and present solutions to complex problems

Steps in Implementation

1. Start by explaining the content of the lesson and the goals of the Mystery Strategy.

2. Engage student interest by presenting a problem to be solved, a question to be answered, or a situation to be explained. Good mysteries often come in the form of "Yes, but why?" questions, which ask students to probe ideas more deeply.

3. Present students with a variety of brief clues and ask them to begin to form hypotheses about the mystery.

4. Ask students to read the clues carefully and organize them into relevant categories. Students should use the categories to test and revise their hypotheses.

5. Call on students to present and defend their hypotheses in front of an audience or in a written paper. Student explanations must be supported with evidence.

6. Hold a reflection session where students can evaluate their explanations and discuss their conclusions in light of the evidence.

Strategy in the Classroom

As part of their exploration of Anthropology, Joyce Wood is having her students study the mystery of the Neanderthals and their disappearance from the Earth. Joyce begins telling her class that today they are going to try to solve a mystery. She introduces her students to the mystery with a brief, image-making session that begins like this:

> OK, I want you all to close your eyes. We're going to try to imagine that we're in another time and in another place. The time is roughly 100,000 years ago, and the place is central Europe. You wake to find yourself in an icy land. You and several members of your tribe are huddled around a fire. You notice that you are all wearing animal skins and it is very cold . . .

After the image-making session, she introduces the mystery:

> Your people number in the thousands in this area, and there is little indication that in less than 65,000 years, there won't be anything left of your people but fossilized bones and a few scant clues pointing to your existence.

"Open your eyes," Joyce instructs her students. "My question to you is, Where did the Neanderthals go? Why did they disappear?"

Joyce then gives her students envelopes that contain clues—brief excerpts from anthropological journals, portions of articles in *The New York Times*, and information from the textbook, including maps and charts of migration and weather patterns, and tables of population size over time for both Neanderthals and Cro-Magnons.

The students form small groups and begin organizing the clues to form initial hypotheses on what happened to the Neanderthals. For instance, here are three clues grouped by one of Joyce's students named Sarah:

- The Neanderthal diet consisted primarily of red meat from large herbivores like deer, wild cattle, and even mammoths. Not surprisingly, most of the Neanderthals' hunting tools were designed for large game.

- Early human ancestors, who lived around the same time as the Neanderthal, had a rather eclectic diet that ranged from small birds and fish, to large deer, to nuts and berries. They had developed tools specially adapted for catching smaller animals, particularly fish, which seems to be completely absent from the Neanderthal diet.

- Whether due to overhunting, a change in migration patterns, or climate change, evidence suggests that large game populations fell considerably just before the Neanderthal became extinct.

From these clues, Sarah realizes that there may have been a connection between the Neanderthal diet and their extinction, so she records the following hypothesis:

- Neanderthals' strict diet of large game and their inability to adapt to hunting smaller animals led to their extinction when large animals became rare.

Based on other clues and evidence, students form a variety of hypotheses:

- ■ Homo sapiens came into conflict with Neanderthals and were directly responsible for their extinction.

- ■ Neanderthals did not become extinct but rather blended into Homo sapien society and mixed their genes with those of modern humans.

Joyce has her students test and refine their hypotheses. As they work, she moves around the room to help those who are having trouble and challenge those who seem overly confident in their hypotheses. The idea, Joyce knows, is to get students to examine evidence from all the clues and to form the hypothesis that can best be supported by the evidence. When students have had time to refine their hypotheses, Joyce asks each group to prepare a presentation on their findings. She encourages her students to create visual aids and handouts to enhance their presentations.

Why the Strategy Works (What the Research Says)

Think back for a moment on the way you were taught to acquire new information. Chances are, the process involved reading a lot of source material (textbooks, encyclopedias, articles, and perhaps primary documents). You were expected to understand and extract information from those documents in order to take an exam or write a paper. In all likelihood, you had little guidance as to how to structure your search or organize the information you were able to find. The whole process probably seemed purposeless, and rarely was your curiosity piqued by the idea that you were solving a real-life mystery. The fact is, instruction students receive in the classroom rarely parallels the way information is gathered by real-world experts and problem solvers (Sternberg, 1985).

In an effort to address this issue while preparing today's students for increasingly demanding state standards, Silver et al. (1996) developed the Mystery strategy. Adapted from Suchman's (1966) Inquiry model, Mystery plays on humans' natural curiosity—that desire to understand our universe and the millions of big and little mysteries that ripple through it. According to Suchman (1966), when students investigate a problem or question under their own impelling curiosity, they are more likely to retain the information they gather along the way because their understanding will be their own.

In addition, recent developments in standards and testing have made the strategy even more important: Document-based questions, in which students must be able to read and interpret multiple documents, are increasingly common on state tests. Because Mystery involves close analysis of multiple source documents, it is a powerful tool for preparing students to meet these demanding state standards.

Do You Hear What I Hear?

Overview

As state and national standards place greater emphasis on literacy skills, teachers are faced with the prospect of developing a skill-based curriculum without cutting into content. Do You Hear What I Hear? (Silver, Strong, & Perini, 2000; Strong & Silver, 1998b) was designed specifically to address this challenge. The strategy sets the bar high, focusing on rigorous texts. Then, through listening, speaking, reading, and writing; through diagnostic coaching; and through regular and sustained commitment to student development, the strategy builds the skills needed to process and respond effectively to these rigorous texts.

Steps in Implementation

1. Leave time to read a short, rigorous text to your students once each week. Read each text twice: once for students to get the gist and once for them to take notes for retelling.

2. Instruct students to pair up and review their notes together. One student puts the notes aside, while the other coaches him or her to a complete retelling. Students then switch roles.

3. Shift from listening to reading by distributing a copy of the text and establishing two to four guiding questions. Guiding questions can focus on vocabulary (e.g., What does *irrational* mean in math?), the meaning of quotations (e.g., What does Sojourner Truth mean when she says, "Ain't I a woman?"), characters' motivations (e.g., Why doesn't Ms. Vasilovna protest when her employer cheats her out of her money?), and themes (e.g., How are extinction and adaptation related according to this article?).

4. Team students up into small, collaborative groups to discuss answers and resolve differences. Observe and coach groups.

5. Establish a writing product based on the reading. The product should be short (one to one-and-a-half pages) and can be in any of these formats: a retelling, a review or argument, a creative response (story, poem, play, etc.), or a personal response.

6. Have students review their products each month, select their best, and work in editor-response groups to collect feedback and revision ideas from their peers.

7. Sit in on editor-response groups and provide coaching. Mark only the selected, revised piece.

Strategy in the Classroom

Amy Silvestri credits the turnaround in her students' reading, speaking, listening, and writing skills to two things: (a) Touchstones (Zeiderman, 1995), a discussion-based program focused on short, challenging texts from around the world, and (b) the creation of Rigorous Mondays. Every Monday is a Rigorous Monday and during Amy's World Literature class, she reads a text from Touchstones aloud to students. Today, she is reading Francis Bacon's essay "About Revenge." She begins by reading aloud the first two lines of the essay: "Revenge is a sort of wild justice. The more people try to take revenge, the more the law should punish them." She asks students to reflect on how Bacon's notion of revenge is similar to or different from their own. Amy then reads the entire essay aloud—twice. The first time, students simply listen, trying to pick up the central idea of the reading. The second time, students take notes on the reading by putting their ideas together so that they can retell the passage to another student.

The students, who are used to this process, pair up, and each student retells the passage to the other student, who serves as a retelling coach. Amy walks around the room, sitting in on various groups and providing extra support and coaching. As she sits in on Eddie and Susan, she is pleased by what she hears:

Eddie: This is the part I had a little trouble with, where Bacon says some kinds of revenge are good even after he's gone through all the reasons revenge is bad.

Susan: Well, he doesn't quite say revenge is good.

Eddie: Right, he says it's "most allowable."

Susan: That's right, and when is it most allowable?

Eddie: Hm, it's when there's no law to, to . . . address a crime. That's when it's most allowable for the victim to resort to revenge.

Susan: Good, so finish your retelling now.

After both students have retold the passage, each pair joins another pair, and they use their copies of "About Revenge" to answer four questions. Today's questions are the following:

■ What are Bacon's purposes in writing this piece?

■ What are his main arguments?

■ What counterarguments does he imagine, and how does he address them?

■ What is the meaning of *private revenge*? (Use specific textual evidence.)

As students formulate and discuss responses, Amy once again circulates to observe students and provide coaching when needed.

When student groups have reached consensus on the questions, Amy gives them their task: *Issues of the Day Magazine* has asked you to write a brief editorial (two to three paragraphs) that responds to Bacon's argument by explaining your position on the role of private revenge in society. They have asked that your article address these questions: Is private revenge justified? If so, when? How should the law react to people who enact revenge plots? Remember what we learned about editorials: State your position, use examples, and be provocative.

Do You Hear What I Hear? happens three Mondays each month. On the fourth Monday of each month, students select their best product for the month and meet in editor-response teams, where they read their selected piece and make revision notes based on the group's feedback. As usual, Amy listens in on these revision sessions to help groups think through the process of providing thoughtful and constructive feedback. This process of selection, feedback collection, and revision helps students produce their best work. But that is only half the story: The same process helps Amy as well. With only one product to mark, Amy is able to provide better feedback and devote more time to diagnosis and coaching.

Why the Strategy Works (What the Research Says)

In their research into the demands the new standards place on the average classroom teacher, Strong and Silver (1998b) found that for a strategy to have a real and positive effect in the classroom and on student performance on state tests, it must meet six essential criteria:

1. It must be easy to implement.

2. It must not require large amounts of planning or marking time.

3. It must allow teachers to work effectively with all students, including struggling students.

4. It must be aligned with state tests and develop the skills identified in state standards.

5. It must engage students in in-depth thinking as well as more routine forms of thought.

6. It must provide manageable opportunities for teachers to diagnose problems and provide coaching.

Do You Hear What I Hear? was designed to respond to these findings. The strategy focuses on key standards-based skills (listening, retelling, note making, using evidence, writing in different genres) and, through repetition and built-in observation and coaching sessions, gives students the time and support they need to develop these skills. In addition, the strategy recognizes the evolutionary nature of deep thought: It begins with simple listening, then progresses through a series of ever-deepening thinking processes: note making, retelling, peer coaching, high-order questions about meanings and themes, synthesis into a written product, and, last, revision. And perhaps best of all, the strategy is effective because it does not place planning or grading burdens on teachers. This, of course, is the point; minimal planning and marking time translate into increased time for diagnosis and coaching—the building blocks of skill development.

Image Making

Overview

Image Making is an essential skill for deep reading, yet it is often taken for granted. The ability to form quick, vivid mental pictures—to see a text unfolding in the mind—is one of the key elements that proficient readers possess but that struggling and average readers lack, preventing them from achieving deep levels of understanding. Image Making breaks down the process of forming mental images into manageable steps so that students can practice and develop the skill more easily.

Steps in Implementation

1. Introduce students to the content and explain the importance of image making in reading.

2. Model the image-making process for students by reading a passage out loud and pausing at key points to accentuate images within the text.

3. Ask students to form pairs to read either together or independently, develop images from the reading, and discuss their images with their partners.

4. Guide students who may be having difficulty by reemphasizing why image making is important, asking questions about their images, or having students use questions to tease out the main ideas in the reading.

5. Encourage students to check their proficiency through class discussion, written descriptions of their images, or by explaining how image making brings reading to life.

Strategy in the Classroom

As part of a unit on endangered species, Lisa Cho is having her seventh graders read a passage on the gray wolf. Before she has her students begin reading, she uses a different reading to conduct a short modeling session with one of her students named Jackie.

Jackie and Lisa sit face to face as Jackie begins to read the passage. Lisa stops Jackie at key points to talk out some of the images she's forming in her head. "OK," says Lisa,

> I heard the phrases "disappearing rapidly," "on guard," "often afraid," and "wary of predators." These words and phrases put an image in my head of a shy and timid creature that is easily startled and is very careful in whatever it does. I picture this deer running away from me, because that is how I remember it is a naturally shy creature.

Lisa then asks some of her students to explain the images that popped into their minds as they listened to Jackie reading. When she is sure her students understand the process of image making, Lisa has them pair off and begin reading their passages on the gray wolf.

"As you read the passage that follows," Lisa explains, "stop and draw sketches that remind you of the big ideas and important details in the reading. Try to avoid using any words in your sketches. Just 'picture' the information."

As her students work, Lisa circulates throughout the class to monitor her students' progress and to help those who may be having trouble. When her students are finished, she holds a class discussion and encourages students to share the images they came up with.

Why the Strategy Works (What the Research Says)

In the twenty-first century, multimedia reigns supreme. It is hard to go a single day without seeing a billboard, a television show, a movie, or a Web site—all of which rely heavily on images and sound to entice and entertain. Most of us are accustomed to processing these images on TV, from advertisements, or in movies. But reading is a different story.

Readers are required to actively create scenes, characters, settings, sounds, and smells in their own minds to bring a text to life. The problem is, visualizing images during reading is a skill many poor and average readers lack (Keene & Zimmermann, 1997). Nonetheless, like most skills, image making is learned and can be taught. In fact, researchers such as Pressley (1977), Sadoski (1985), and Gambrell and Bales (1986) found that, in little more than half an hour, teachers can teach students how to create effective images while they read.

Compare and Contrast

Overview

Whenever we encounter new information, we naturally assimilate it in terms of how it is similar to and different from what we already know. This strategy, Compare and Contrast, taps into students' natural inclination to examine and classify information by providing two related concepts or readings, which they analyze comparatively. Using focused criteria, students learn how to structure their reading to determine key attributes and the similarities and differences between two or more concepts or texts.

Steps in Implementation

1. Review the process of comparing and contrasting with students by briefly modeling with two common objects or well-known events.

2. Establish the purpose for comparing the content you have chosen (e.g., How will comparing and contrasting these items deepen our understanding?).

3. List criteria for analyzing the characteristics of each item independently (e.g., What are its parts? What is its function? How does it work?) and ask students to use these criteria to examine each item separately.

4. After students have generated two lists of characteristics, show them how to use an organizer (see the sample reproducible organizer, Resource 4.2) to examine what makes each item unique and what characteristics they may share.

5. Take time to conduct a class discussion on the similarities and differences students noted. Discussion can be sparked by asking questions leading to debate, such as What is the central difference between these two items? Why? Are they more similar or more different? What conclusions can we draw? What might be some causes or possible effects of a particular difference?

6. Encourage students to reflect on their performance during the strategy, and guide them toward becoming independent learners by encouraging them to apply the strategy on their own during independent reading.

Strategy in the Classroom

George Russell wants his Economics students to understand the two major economic models of the twentieth century: socialism and capitalism. George begins the lesson by generating a list of criteria with his students that will focus their attention on essential characteristics of each economic model. After students have recorded the criteria in their notebooks, he begins:

"Today, we are going to be comparing and contrasting socialism and capitalism in an effort to understand the similarities and differences between the two economic systems.

"Keep in mind," George continues, "that following your analysis of these two systems, you are going to design an efficient mixed economy for a new nation."

Figure 4.4. Student Notes

Socialism	Criteria	Capitalism
Government controls ownership of land and many manufacturing operations.	Ownership	
Personal income regulated to be relatively equal across the board. Economic freedom limited in favor of limited class conflict.	Personal income/Economic freedom	
Government regulates most institutions. All land owned by state. Most services and manufacturing provided primarily by the state.	Role of government	

Students are given two texts, one explaining Karl Marx's economic theory and another describing the ideas of capitalist theorists, such as Adam Smith and Milton Friedman. Students read both texts and begin determining the key attributes of each economic system according to the criteria they recorded in their notebooks (see Figure 4.4).

George's students then form small groups and share and refine their attributes to make sure everyone has understood the readings. When his students have finished refining their notes, George addresses them again: "Now, in teams of four, use the visual organizer I am handing out to list the similarities and differences between socialism and capitalism based on the same criteria you have in your notes." (See Resource 4.2.)

After the groups have completed the Compare and Contrast organizer, George leads them in a discussion. He knows that when it comes to comparing and contrasting, good discussions do three things: They explore the causes and effects of significant differences, they encourage students to examine the implications of similarities, and they ask students to consider whether the things being compared are more alike or different. Once the discussion in George's class is complete, students use their analysis of the similarities and differences between the two economic systems to create a mixed economic model for a new nation, based on the greatest strengths of both systems. George asks his students to keep the following goals in mind as they create their new economic model:

- Encourage new citizens to become part of the new nation.

- Establish a place in the world economy.

- Achieve the highest standard of living in the world at the lowest cost to the new citizens.

Why the Strategy Works (What the Research Says)

Teachers seek to equip their students with the tools that enable them to become independent learners. On the road to student independence, however, it is easy to overlook essential tools that seem too basic to warrant close attention. According to educational researcher Robert Marzano (1992), this is why many teachers gloss over comparing and contrasting: It is not that teachers don't acknowledge the ability to identify the similarities and differences as an essential skill, but that they see the skill as almost too basic to teach. Yet there is clearly a need for direct teaching of comparing and contrasting as a thinking and reading skill, as recent research shows that most American students lack the basic skills needed to make sophisticated comparisons (Mullis, Owen, & Phillips, 1990).

A great advantage of the Compare and Contrast strategy is that it develops the skills students need to extract important information from a reading (or readings) without requiring significant prior knowledge of the subject or content. This acquisition of sophisticated comparison skills occurs for students in three stages:

1. First, students learn to extract the critical attributes from each reading or concept based on given criteria.

2. Second, they learn how to set these attributes against each other so that the important similarities and differences emerge.

3. Last, over time, students learn to form their own criteria and to use these criteria to make thoughtful comparisons across content areas.

A blank, reproducible organizer for comparing and contrasting is given in Resource 4.2.

Resource 4.2. Organizer for Compare and Contrast

Differences	**Differences**

Similarities

Applications to Specific Content Areas

Reading and Interpreting Primary Documents in Social Studies

One of the exciting aspects of teaching and learning history is that primary documents collapse huge gaps of time, offering us real, unclouded glimpses into the mindsets of people who lived hundreds or thousands of years before us. But the predominance of primary documents and the importance of making sure students know how to read and interpret them poses a special challenge to the social studies teacher. One of the most effective ways of building this essential skill in students is to use the structure of interpretive strategies, such as Reading for Meaning or Compare and Contrast.

For example, Lester McManus uses Reading for Meaning to help students read and interpret three primary documents related to the feudal economic system of the Middle Ages: a statement by a lord declaring his rights and responsibilities, a set of regulations describing the limits between a lord and his vassal, and an oath sworn by a vassal to his lord. Thus, using a typical Reading for Meaning organizer, students collect evidence for and against focused statements designed to surface the central ideas uniting the three documents (see Figure 4.5).

A Problem-Based Approach to Mathematical and Scientific Thinking

Deep reading in subjects such as algebra, geometry, physics, and chemistry means being able to combine the skills of inferential reading with quantitative problem solving, which is often integrated into the text. Too often, though, students try to jump to instant solutions rather than thinking problems through. Do You See What I See? (Strong & Silver, 1998a) is a strategy that curtails impulsivity and develops students' problem-solving skills through presolution planning, regular practice, and cooperative learning techniques. It works like this:

1. Devote one class period a week to exploring complex and nonroutine problems connected with current or past math topics (e.g., Problem-Solving Friday).

2. Read the problem aloud to your students, twice. During the first reading, ask students to take notes on the relevant information. During the second reading, ask them to create a sketch representing the problem using numbers or letters (but no words) where appropriate.

3. Provide students with a written description of the problem, and ask them to revise their notes *but not solve the problem.*

Figure 4.5. Middle Ages Organizer

The "contracts" between lords and vassals were controlled completely by the lord.	
Evidence for	Evidence against

The "contracts" between lords and vassals were cold, hard, "legalistic" arrangements.	
Evidence for	Evidence against

The "contracts" between lords and vassals were mutually beneficial.	
Evidence for	Evidence against

4. Create small, collaborative groups of three to four students and ask the teams to share their information. Then, ask them to define what the problem is asking for, develop a plan to solve the problem, *but not solve the problem.*

5. As students work, circulate, listening to and observing their approaches. Ask questions but do not attempt to provide answers or hints. Select two or three students with different approaches to lay out their plans to the class while the class questions and critiques.

6. Assign the problem for homework. Students need to solve the problem individually and submit written justifications for their approaches. Stu-

Figure 4.6. Algebra Problem

A series of rectangular rods are stacked on top of each other and staggered by 1cm. The rods are all the same size. The length, width, and height of one of the rods are 12cm, 4cm, and 4cm respectively. Determine the total surface area and volume of the stacked rods when the number of rods shown in the table is used. Use the patterns of the progressive surface areas and volumes to find a general formula for the surface area and volume when n rods are used.

Number of Rods	Surface Area	Volume
1		
2		
3		
4		
5		
n		

dents do three problems like this a month, then select their best effort, meet in an editor-response group, and revise and publish their work. The teacher marks only the one published piece.

For example, Keyshawn Wright uses Do You See What I See? in his Algebra classroom. A typical problem from his classroom is shown in Figure 4.6.

Socratic Seminars and Discussion Groups in English: Helping Students Lead Their Own Discussions

In developing the skills for reading beyond the information given, students need opportunities to communicate, explore, and refine ideas with other students. Students often learn essential skills, such as explaining, making claims, and using evidence orally, and then transfer these skills to their reading and writing. Whole-class discussions, although useful, are sometimes flat, are too often teacher directed, and may tend to wander away from the text, with students simply voicing opinions without evidence. Socratic Seminar (Adler, 1982), or student-led discussions centered on a text or a set of thematically linked texts, is one way to address the failings of traditional whole-class discussion. The strategy is a powerful way to deepen discussions in any classroom; it is especially useful in English, where opinions without textual evidence and statements like "That's just how I feel" are most commonly heard.

The steps for conducting a Socratic Seminar follow, along with a running example from the classroom of American Literature teacher Carla Domingo:

1. Assign a reading or thematically linked group of readings. Ask students to take notes that will help them understand and talk about the central issues in their readings.

   Carla wants her students to understand how a single piece of literature functions in various ways. She chooses Charlotte Perkins Gilman's "The Yellow Wallpaper," which is part of their two-month study of American short stories. Students also read Gilman's "Why I Wrote 'The Yellow Wallpaper'" along with two short pieces of literary criticism. She asks students to take notes on how the story functions as a psychological study, a horror story, and an argument for social reform.

2. Share the criteria for the seminar with students before they begin.

   Carla and her students discuss the four criteria for thoughtful seminars: preparation, understanding of content, participation, and use of evidence.

3. Arrange the classroom in a circle, and begin the seminar by asking a provocative, sparking question.

   Carla begins her seminar by asking: "Do you think the narrator of the story is crazy?"

4. Allow students to exchange their ideas about the question. Students do not need to raise their hands to respond; the only rules are that they must let each other speak, must show respect to all speakers' positions, and must use evidence from the texts whenever they make a claim.

   Carla sits in the circle and becomes a participant in the seminar. She makes sure that students know they are running the seminar and intervenes only once: When Jason tries to dominate the discussion by insisting, without evidence, that the narrator is insane, Carla says, "That's an interesting position, and you sure are passionate about it. Tell us what evidence you can find in the story to back up your ideas." At other points, when Carla would normally intervene (for example, during a period of extended silence), she lets the students work it out. Although this is awkward for her at first, she knows it tells students that they are responsible for what happens in the classroom.

5. Use a few focusing questions throughout the seminar to keep the discussion from drifting too far from the central issues and a closing question to synthesize the seminar.

> As she listens and participates, Carla periodically poses a new focusing question. For today's seminar, she poses a total of three focusing questions: the opening question plus two more (Is the story supposed to scare the reader? What is Gilman arguing for?). Near the end of the seminar, Carla presents the closing question: Is the story mostly a psychological study, a horror story, or a social argument?

6. Present the final task, along with the criteria for success.

> Carla wants students to reflect on the seminar and then to develop a thesis essay that argues whether "The Yellow Wallpaper" is mostly a psychological study, a horror story, or a social argument. Before students begin, the class reviews the criteria for thesis essays: clarity of position, effective use of evidence, responsiveness to counterarguments, and mastery of writing conventions.

Strategies for Struggling Readers

As in textbook reading, or gist-oriented reading, students may experience difficulty at three distinct stages of the reading: before reading, when students have difficulty bringing their prior knowledge to bear on a new text; during reading, when students have difficulty reading actively and with purpose; and after reading, when students have difficulty distilling or elaborating on what they have read. Thus, the suggestions provided at the end of Chapter 1 can all be applied to inferential reading as well as to its more literal cousin.

Beyond the pre-, during-, and post-reading paradigm outlined in Chapter 1, four other techniques are especially useful in helping readers who are having difficulty reading beyond the information given:

1. Help students get the gist first. As Benjamin Bloom (1956) taught the educational world with his influential *Taxonomy of Education Objectives*, understanding is stratified. Higher-order thinking skills, such as application, analysis, synthesis, and critical evaluation, are dependent on lower-order thinking skills, such as recall and developing a working understanding of central ideas. What this means is that if we expect students to become higher-order readers, we must first be sure they know how to get the gist of what they read. Use of reading strategies, such as Text Structure, Graphic Organizers, Peer Reading, and Collaborative Summarizing (see Chapter 1), will help students develop the foundation they need in order to think more deeply about texts.

2. Don't neglect the importance of image making. A great deal of research shows that image making is a critical part of the proficient reader's toolbox. Neglecting this skill and focusing exclusively on more analytical skills, such as using evidence and comparative reading, robs texts of their cinematic quality and denies many students the opportunities they need to bring reading to life. For the struggling reader who lacks interest or who is easily frustrated by analytical tasks, use the power of Image Making as a natural springboard into more critical reading.

3. Use Information Search as a way to build critical reading skills. Information Search (Silver & Strong, 1994) is a strategy that helps students access their prior knowledge and then organize that knowledge into a conceptual framework they can use to build comprehension. Specifically, the strategy teaches students how to

- Use their memories, intuitions, and personal feelings to "crack" a reading

- Actively seek out information

- Visually mark a text to determine the relevance of specific information

- Elaborate on how their understanding has been changed by the reading

Information Search moves through four basic steps:

1. *Select a reading and identify the main subtopics.* (To build deeper purpose into student reading, you may want to convert the subtopics into questions.) For example, Harold Longacre teaches sociology and wants students to explore the scientific basis for sociology. Using an article titled "Sociology: Hard or Soft Science?" Harold converts the main subtopics into these four questions:
   - What investigative methods do sociologists use?
   - What investigative methods do scientists use?
   - What's the difference between hard and soft science?
   - Why do people argue over the distinction between hard and soft science?

2. *Ask students to identify what they know, what they think they know, what they want to know, and how they feel about each subtopic.* Then, using the class's input, create a comprehensive map like the one shown in Figure 4.7.

3. *Teach students how to use reader's punctuation to search for information and connect their reading to the map.* A simple set of reader's punctuation might be
   ! = This is new information.
   – = This is information that conflicts with the map.
   + = This is information that agrees with the map.
   ? = I have a question about this.

4. *After students have read and marked their text, ask them to synthesize their new understanding by creating a revised map or an organizer of their own.*

Figure 4.7. Comprehensive Map of Sociology: Hard or Soft Science?

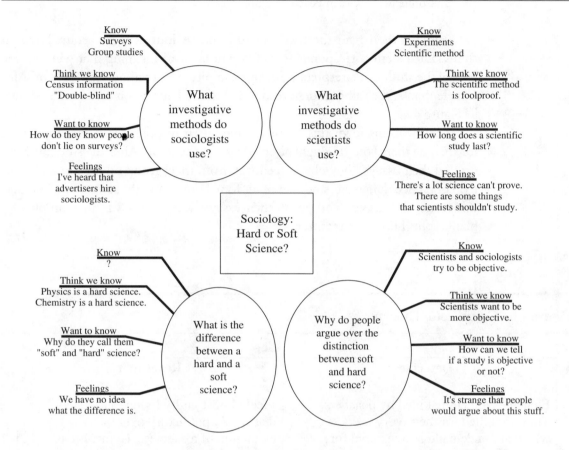

4. Use Four Thought to help students build sophisticated interpretations step by step. Good interpretations tend to be layered, combining clear description, critical thinking, personal response—even imagination, speculation, and problem solving. The problem for many readers—especially struggling readers—is that they have difficulty managing and differentiating between these layers of meaning. As a result, many students' interpretations amount to simple summaries without insight (single-layer interpretations) or headlong rushes into the topic in which several aspects of the text are mentioned, or reacted to, or described, or speculated on, but few or none are carried through to a meaningful end (multilayer interpretations but no sense of how to manage the layers). This problem is exacerbated by the fact that new open-response items on state tests are calling for ever-increasing levels of sophistication in students' explanations and interpretations.

Four Thought (Silver et al., 2001) leads students through a step-by-step process of building high-quality interpretations. The strategy begins with students' being introduced to the topic or title of the reading and then generating prereading associations based on what they know, what they think they know, or how they feel about the topic. For example, before reading an article on endangered elephants in Africa, one student generated the following associations:

Africa		awful	habitat	extinct
hunters		greed	ecosystem	
environment	Green Peace	vulnerable		

Students then read the text and respond to four separate Four Thought stems. Each stem corresponds to a different layer of meaning that will become part of the student's interpretation. For example, after reading the article on African elephants, the same student responded to the Four Thought stems as shown in Figure 4.8.

Next, working in groups, students share their responses and exchange ideas for turning their Four Thoughts into essays on the topic. After the students have drafted their essays, they obtain feedback from their group on their essays' clarity, coherence, language, and use of all four Four Thought stems. Students use this feedback to revise and polish their essays. Resource 4.3 is an example of a blank Four Thought organizer.

Figure 4.8. Greg's Four Thoughts

Describe it	React to it
Elephants are being killed by poachers. They are killed for their ivory tusks, which are in demand as a material for making jewelry.	I feel almost guilty living in a society that would put luxury over the extinction of a species. To me, life is more precious than ivory or art or profit, and I would like to know what gives people the right to hunt a species to virtual extinction for a mere luxury.
Analyze it	**Solve it**
The poachers' livelihoods depend on ivory. The poachers who kill the wild African elephants do so to earn money to feed and clothe themselves and their families. However, is poaching the only answer to their economic needs?	The first step in solving this problem is to educate the public. There are millions of people who have never even heard of the wild African elephant. If they knew about this situation, I'm sure many of them would be sympathetic. The second step would be to find another way for the poachers to make money. Maybe they could set up government jobs for them to turn to instead of killing.

SOURCE: Silver et al. (2001); reprinted with permission.

Resource 4.3. Four Thought Organizer

Four Thought Organizer

Topic:_____

Prereading Associations:

```



```

Four Thought:

Describe it	React to it
Analyze it	**Solve it**

Alternative Four Thought Stems:

Instead of *describing it*, students can *define it* or *sequence it*.

Instead of *analyzing it*, students can *compare it* or *prove it*.

Instead of *solving it*, students can *visualize/metaphorize it* or *improve it*.

Instead of *reacting to it*, students can *be it* or *teach it*.

CHAPTER

5 Turning Questions Into Quests

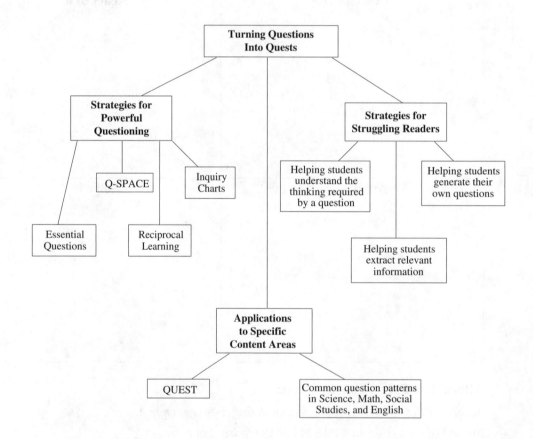

Then joy awakened in that dwelling when the king knew that the good Sir Gawain
was come, for he deemed it gain. King Arthur kissed the knight, and the queen also,
and many valiant knights sought to embrace him. They asked him how he had fared,
and he told them all that had chanced to him—the adventure of the chapel, the fashion
of the knight, the love of the lady—at last of the lace. He showed them the wound in
the neck which he won for his disloyalty at the hand of the knight, the blood flew to
his face for shame as he told the tale.

So goes the hero's return in *Sir Gawain and the Green Knight*, one of the greatest examples of quest literature in the English language. The idea of the quest is that the hero goes on a journey in search of something—the Holy Grail, a mysterious green knight, a magical place supposedly invested with great power. But what we find in almost all quest literature is that attainment of that goal is not the key element. If the object is found at all, it turns out to be different—usually less impressive—than expected. What is key is that the quest, with its tests, adventures, and interactions with others, allows the hero to learn essential lessons about himself and about the world. Through the quest, the hero becomes a progressively better knight.

It's really the same way when it comes to questions. A question can serve as a quest—an invitation to journey into a text. The point of this invitation is not to turn students into detail-fixated hunters who find precise bits of information but are unable to engage deeply with the text. Rather, the point is to ask ourselves, How can questions turn students into better and deeper readers?

Think about it. What are the effects of beginning a unit on statistics focused on the questions, "Do statistics tell the whole story?" and "What's the difference between using statistics and abusing statistics?" How would the inherent mystery of a question such as "How did a ragtag militia of untrained soldiers defeat the most powerful army in the world?" illuminate a set of readings on the American Revolution? Do you think questions such as "Are there limits to scientific endeavors?" and "Should progress be driven by ethics, economics, or sheer possibility?" would provoke students to think and read a *New York Times* article on the human genome project more deeply? How about, "Do readers find important ideas or make them up?" as a frame for investigating a set of short stories by writers such as Anton Chekhov, Ernest Hemingway, or Raymond Carver, who convey ideas through implications and deceptively simple dialogue? Even more fact-oriented questions, such as "How are linear equations used in the real world?" or "What kinds of techniques do reporters use to make their writing clear and interesting?" can have a profound effect on student interest and motivation.

Questions do five things for readers:

1. They activate students' prior knowledge.

2. They establish a purpose for reading.

3. They indicate the type of thinking that students will need to apply to the reading (e.g., Will I be looking to develop a position? Solve a mystery? Find specific information? Compare and contrast two texts?).

4. They serve as a filter for reading, helping students to determine what is important (Does this information help me to answer the question?) and what is not.

5. They encourage students to engage in postreading thinking and to notice their growth as learners by comparing their new understanding of the question with their prereading understanding.

In this chapter, you will learn to harness the power of four different kinds of questions:

■ *Topic-specific questions* tend to be literal in nature, focusing student attention on key ideas and supporting details. Here are some examples:

What developments made Columbus's journey possible?

How do you construct a sound mathematical proof?

In what ways did Beethoven expand the form of the symphony?

How do cells transform food into energy?

■ *Essential questions* help students to think critically by connecting content in a particular unit to deep and pervasive issues in the discipline. Good essential questions can never be answered fully; they always spur discussion, debate, the marshaling of evidence, and negotiation between multiple perspectives. For example,

What if organisms couldn't adapt?

How do linear equations help us to understand and interpret the world around us?

Could America have remained neutral during World War I?

What makes a good survey in a sociological study?

■ *Enduring questions* are broader than essential questions in that they are designed to be returned to throughout the year. In this way, they serve as the spine for yearlong inquiry in a discipline. Some examples follow:

How is the multicultural experience reflected in the work of American authors?

Can war ever be just?

Does good art need to be beautiful?

How does form affect function?

Often, enduring questions are focused through supporting questions that structure student inquiry. For example, the question "Can war ever be just?" might be supported by, "Are the causes just? Is the conduct just? Are the consequences just?"

- *Student questions* are the questions students create themselves to help them make sense and meaning of the texts they read. Student questions can take the form of topic-specific questions, essential questions, or enduring questions.

In this chapter, we present four questioning strategies:

- *Essential Questions* unite all the readings that make up a unit or course of study, providing a broad, inquiry-based focus for learning.

- *Q-SPACE* helps deepen student comprehension through effective classroom questioning practices.

- *Reciprocal Teaching* teaches students how to develop and use questions to manage difficult texts.

- *I-Charts* focus on the connection between questions and research.

At the end of the chapter, we will explore the most common question patterns in the disciplines of science, math, social studies, and English, and we will present tips and strategies for helping struggling readers tap into the power of questions.

Strategies for Powerful Questioning

Essential Questions

Overview

When learning is unfocused and lacks clear purpose, students respond negatively, often becoming bored, unmotivated, and confused. Supported by Essential Questions, however, learning becomes not just focused and goal oriented but also questlike in nature—a search for the deeper meanings that give life to the discipline. We call these questions *essential* because they steer students toward the

Figure 5.1 Three Essential Questions on Heat

Why do we need a theory of heat?

What are the advantages and disadvantages of different theories of heat?

What aspects of ordinary life can only be explained through a theory of heat?

central ideas of a discipline while respecting student diversity by allowing a wide variety of responses and insights.

Steps in Implementation

1. Fashion questions so that they have universal appeal, enabling every student in the class to relate to them.

2. Remember that these questions should not spark yes or no answers or even short answers. They should, however, spark deep thought, varied opinions, curiosity, and new questions and should guide student learning.

3. Once the questions have been created, encourage students to use them as a springboard for ideas as well as a filter for notes and answers during reading.

4. Throughout the unit, have students check their progress by frequently returning to the essential questions to test their understanding of the content.

5. During synthesis activities, use the essential questions to focus learning by making sure the activity is responsive to one or more of the essential questions.

Strategy in the Classroom

This week, Adell Norwich is opening a unit on heat. She begins by handing her students a sheet with three essential questions for the unit in bold type (see Figure 5.1).

Throughout the unit and as they read and conduct inquiries, Adell's students will use these questions to focus their thinking, synthesize their findings, and generate new questions. Before they begin, however, Adell notices looks of confusion on some students' faces.

Adell: I see some confused looks. Marsha, do you have a question?

Marsha: Well, how are we supposed to know why we need a theory of heat when we don't even know the theory of heat?

Adell: I was waiting for someone to ask that. What Marsha is noticing is that, in order to attempt to answer these essential questions, we're going to need more specific questions to focus our reading and research. I think Marsha has already given us one specific question, "What are the theories of heat?" Can anyone give me another specific question that we'll need to answer before we can answer the essential question?

Together, Adell and her students generate a list of about ten topic-specific questions to help students focus on specific information so they will be able to speak intelligently about the essential questions. The topic-specific questions that Adell's class generates seek clear, verifiable information, unlike the essential questions, which are more open-ended.

As students acquire new information throughout the unit, they check the answers they find to the topic-specific questions and begin to form ideas about how to answer the essential questions.

Later on in the week, during lab time, Adell conducts a synthesis activity where she has students perform experiments that will help them answer the essential question "What aspects of ordinary life can only be explained through a theory of heat?" For homework, Adell has her students write a two-page essay that addresses this essential question and that uses the information they've gathered from their readings and the data they obtained from the lab.

Why the Strategy Works (What the Research Says)

Many schools have fallen victim to so-called content-driven curricula. These programs of study are so strongly centered on the mastery of content that the needs of students as individual learners are often ignored. In an effort to shift emphasis away from a purely content-based approach that often fails to engage students or promote lasting understanding, researchers such as Martin-Kniep (2000) and Wiggins and McTighe (1998) tout the value of essential questions.

An essential question serves as a lighthouse, guiding student learning through a range of content and preventing students from getting lost. Wiggins and McTighe (1998) point to three basic characteristics that are germane to all essential questions:

1. They get at the core concepts of the discipline.

2. They continually and naturally emerge during the learning process.

3. They help surface new questions.

It is important to note that these three characteristics show not only what essential questions are but also what they are not. They should never be easily answerable, and they do not have yes or no or even short answers. Essential questions are meant to be provocative, to spark a genuine interest by allowing students to use the content to form meaningful interpretations. Often, essential questions raise many more questions as their answers are sought.

There have been some questions raised by teachers and researchers alike as to whether essential questions are sometimes too broad for students to use in extracting specific information. In such cases, it may be necessary to develop topic-specific questions. These are questions that are more closely related to particular content and should serve as doorways to the essential questions. As Wiggins and McTighe (1998) are careful to note, there is some gray area as to when a question is essential and when it is topic specific. What is most important to keep in mind, however, are the larger purposes of the questioning process in general:

- To focus student learning

- To spark student interest

- To provide a guiding light for learning

Q-SPACE

Overview

In the same way that every question seeks an answer, every answer seeks a response. The technique teachers use to pose questions and respond to students' answers plays an important role in determining the extent and kinds of thinking students will use when engaging with a text. Q-SPACE, which takes its name from the first letters of its steps, seeks to deepen and strengthen students' thinking about the texts they read by

- Providing longer response time

- Probing, accepting, and helping to clarify responses

- Encouraging elaboration on responses

Steps in Implementation

1. *Question:* Pose a content-specific question for students to answer. Encourage students to take out pen and paper for taking notes during the Q-SPACE session.

2. *S*ilence: Remain silent after posing the question to allow time for students to generate ideas. Maintain eye contact, and let your demeanor show that you're interested in what students have to say.

3. *P*robe: Respond to answers with questions about the process of answering (e.g., How did you arrive at that answer? Can you give us any concrete examples?). The goal is to make the thinking process visible to students. Even if students' answers are cursory or incomplete, use probing to help them develop their thinking.

4. *A*ccept: Communicate to students the positive aspects of their answers, for answers are provisional and, therefore, both acceptable ("That's very interesting.") and doubtful ("We need to look at this a little further.").

5. *C*larify and correct: Aid students in making their answers clear and useful by using three basic techniques:

   ■ When the answer is incorrect, state the question for which the answer is correct.

   ■ When the answer is jumbled or confused, restate the answer or ask the student to restate it.

   ■ When the answer is irrelevant, use focusing questions to put students back on track.

6. *E*laborate: Encourage students to look past answers to see where they may lead. You can ask students to build on their answers by adding more data, further examples, or new specifics, or you can ask students to build something new in the form of a tentative generalization that explains a variety of data.

Strategy in the Classroom

Lisa Hibner is in the first week of a unit on World War I with her eleventh-grade World History class. They are studying the causes of World War I, and today, Lisa gives her students three short primary documents to examine. The first two are brief letters exchanged between Francis Joseph, Emperor of Austria-Hungary, and Kaiser Wilhelm II of Germany concerning the annexation of Bosnia-Herzegovina. The third document is the declaration of the annexation to the people of Bosnia-Herzegovina.

To begin, Lisa asks her students to read the three documents and then begins questioning and discussion using Q-SPACE:

OK, please take out some paper and a pen so that you can take notes as we discuss. The main question I would like to ask is, Why does Francis Joseph write Wilhelm II to inform him of the annexation?

Lisa pauses for a few seconds to see if any hands go up. When none do, she asks a specific student.

Lisa: Jeffrey, do you have any thoughts?

Jeffrey looks back over the documents for a few seconds before offering a response.

Jeffrey: Uh . . . well, Francis Joseph and Wilhelm are friends, so he wants to make sure what he's doing is OK with him.

Lisa: Do you mean that Francis Joseph wants to make sure the annexation is OK with Kaiser Wilhelm?

Jeffrey: Yes.

Lisa: What leads you to believe that they're friends?

Jeffrey: Uh . . . well (pauses for a few seconds before continuing), the letter begins "My dear friend" and ends "Your faithful friend," and he talks about the "close relationship that unites us as friends."

Lisa: Excellent. Does anyone think that Francis Joseph and the Kaiser are more than just social friends? Is there a political relationship between them and their countries? Kelly?

Kelly: They're also allies.

Lisa pauses to see if Kelly has finished her thought and invites her, with a nod, to continue.

Kelly: So Francis Joseph wants to make sure that he will not offend his ally Kaiser Wilhelm and Germany by annexing Bosnia-Herzegovina.

Lisa: Very good. So Francis Joseph is making sure that he has the Kaiser's support?

Kelly: Right.

Lisa: OK, Alan, what do you see happening when Austria-Hungary eventually declares war on Bosnia-Herzegovina?

Alan looks down at the documents and then looks up, a little confused.

Lisa: What do you think Germany will do?

Alan: Probably help Francis Joseph because they're allies.

Lisa: I think that's a very good guess.

Lisa then asks her students to form small groups to discuss how Francis Joseph's letter to the Kaiser and his declaration of the annexation to Bosnia-Herzegovina differ in tone. Students discuss and take notes while Lisa walks around the room and monitors their discussions. When they've finished, she asks her students to make predictions about what they think will happen next and how they think the people of Bosnia-Herzegovina feel about the annexation.

At the end of the lesson, Lisa conducts a reflection session with her students. She asks them how the use of primary documents helps to understand history. She also asks about the process—how questions and discussions help build understanding.

Why the Strategy Works (What the Research Says)

The classic model of questioning and answering—a model most familiar to us from standardized testing, end-of-chapter questions, and the like—poses a single question to which there is only one correct answer. What this model ignores, however, is that questions—especially good questions—are provisional and that deep thinking is developed when students' ideas are brought to the surface and then refined through interaction with other thoughts, ideas, and questions. When a question is answered, new questions spring forth, yielding new responses, and so on.

This evolutionary process of deepening thought through questioning and answering is central to Q-SPACE (Strong, Hanson, & Silver, 1995). Every student's answer becomes a building block from which the class can construct a better, more meaningful answer through feedback and further questions.

The strategy has been designed to maximize the power of classroom questioning by incorporating three key elements:

1. *Building in wait time:* As Rowe (1972) and Lake (1973) discovered, three to five seconds of silence after questions has a significant impact on students' answers. Wait time makes students more confident in their responses and enables them to justify their ideas with evidence.

2. *Probing, accepting, and clarifying students' answers:* Students are naturally insecure when approaching unfamiliar content. However, as Costa (1991) points out, teacher behaviors, such as clarifying, probing, and paraphrasing students' answers, enable students to organize and refine their thoughts and help them gain confidence in themselves and their thinking.

3. *Elaborating on ideas to create new understandings:* When asked to elaborate on their own answers and thinking, students are better able to engage in activities that proficient readers perform, such as rereading a text, correcting misunderstandings, and making and monitoring predictions.

Reciprocal Teaching

Overview

Holding to the adage "to teach is to learn twice over," Reciprocal Teaching (Palinscar & Brown, 1984) invites students to take on teaching practices not always familiar to them in the dynamics of the classroom. This multiple-strategy approach is designed to help students develop the skills most often identified as those used by proficient readers when processing difficult texts: asking questions, managing new vocabulary, summarizing, and predicting.

Steps in Implementation

1. Model with students each of the skills central to the strategy: asking questions, managing new vocabulary, summarizing, and predicting.

2. Engage students in Think Aloud sessions (as you perform a skill, think out loud to reveal your thinking process) to model how they might use the strategies when approaching a difficult text.

3. Allow one student to serve as teacher for a particular passage in the reading by asking other students questions about the text.

4. Support the student teacher by reminding him or her to focus the class on detail questions, important ideas, difficult vocabulary, summarizing the passage, and making predictions about what will come next.

5. Over time, shift responsibility for discussions to students. The goal is to develop students' abilities as self-sufficient readers, where they stop themselves to ask and answer questions that will help them understand a text.

Strategy in the Classroom

Kathy Goldman and her seventh-grade math class are beginning a unit on geometry. As part of her effort to bring more rigorous content into her classroom, Kathy has chosen the beginning of Book I of Euclid's *Elements* for a reciprocal-teaching lesson. This is not the first time she has used the strategy, so she skips the introductory modeling sessions that her students are familiar with and jumps right into the reading, which begins with four definitions:

1. A point is that of which there is no part.

2. A line is a breadthless length.

3. A line's ends are points.

4. A straight line is one that lies evenly with the points on itself.

After her students have read the first four of Euclid's definitions, Kathy appoints Rosa to act as the first student teacher.

Kathy (to Rosa, who is the "teacher"): OK, Rosa, what questions would you like to ask the class?

Rosa: Um . . . How many parts does a point have?

Jason: None. Zero parts.

Kathy: That was a very good question, Rosa. What you just asked is called a detail question. A detail question asks for specific information about a particular part of the reading. The answer is usually quick and simple, as Jason showed us. Now, Rosa, can you ask a generalizing question?

Rosa: Well, first I have a question about a word.

Kathy: Great. Sometimes before you can ask a generalizing or a detail question, you have to understand what certain words mean, so go ahead and ask.

Rosa: What does the word *breadthless* mean?

Kathy: Do you know what width is?

Rosa: Isn't that how wide something is?

Kathy: Exactly, and width and breadth are the same thing, so if something is breadthless?

David: Then it has no breadth, and that means that it has no width.

Kathy: Right. Boy, you people are good. OK, now do you think you can ask a generalizing question, Rosa?

Rosa: Sure. What is a line?

Amy: A line ends in points . . . is made up of many points . . . and, um, has no width.

Kathy: Great! You see how Amy had to read all four points carefully in order to give that answer. Great job. Rosa, can you give us a summary of Euclid's first four definitions?

Rosa: Um . . . OK . . . A point is something with no parts that makes up the ends of a line. A line has no width and lies evenly between the points that make it up.

Kathy: Excellent! You got all the important ideas without using too many words. Nice job. OK, I think we're ready to move on, but before we do, Rosa, do you have any predictions as to what we'll encounter next in Euclid's definitions?

Rosa: Well, he started with points and then said points make up a line, so now maybe he'll talk about what lines make up.

Kathy: I think that's a pretty good prediction. Euclid seems to be building on concepts from basic ones, like points, to increasingly complex ones, like lines. Let's get a new teacher for the next four definitions and see if Rosa is correct . . .

Why the Strategy Works (What the Research Says)

Reciprocal Teaching is a multiple strategy approach designed to help students develop four key skills: asking questions, summarizing, predicting, and managing new and challenging vocabulary (Palinscar & Brown 1984; Pressley, Woloshyn, & Associates, 1995).

Modeling and Reciprocal Teaching go hand in hand. In Reciprocal Teaching, the proficient-reader strategies must be modeled to students before the strategy can be fully implemented. One of the most important things to keep in mind when engaging students in the Reciprocal Teaching strategy is that the strategy is designed to help teachers determine what aspects of the reading process are giving students difficulty. When students experience difficulty in summarizing, for instance, the teacher should play a more active role by serving as a coach. Conversely, when student comprehension is high, the support from the teacher should be gradually reduced. This way, student confidence and independence grow with each use of the strategy.

Inquiry Charts (I-Charts)

Overview

At the heart of good research lie good questions—rich and provocative inquiries into a subject. Forming questions for research and then using these questions to manage and organize the research process are the crucial skills developed by I-Charts.

Steps in Implementation

1. Ask students to generate critical thinking questions about a topic. (Depending on students' comfort with this process, you may need to begin with whole-class or group work in formulating questions for research.)

2. Distribute I-Chart organizers, and have students record their question(s) in the appropriate spaces.

3. Encourage students to think about, discuss, and record what they already know about each question.

4. Allow time for independent research from multiple sources (books, articles, CD-ROMs, the Internet, etc.). Students record the appropriate infor-

mation from each source onto their I-Charts and keep proper bibliographic references for each source.

5. After the research, encourage students to reflect by noting variations among sources, discussing how their prior knowledge has changed or evolved, and thinking about how and why different sources contain different information.

6. Ask students to develop a cohesive summary of their findings.

7. Set up Writers' Clubs for students to work with their peers in converting their I-Charts into drafts, giving and receiving feedback, and revising the drafts. Make sure students have clear criteria for evaluating their own and their peers' work.

Strategy in the Classroom

Gabriel Booth knows how important research skills are to the academic success of college students. He also knows that many high school students lack a systematic approach to developing research questions, collecting sources, gathering relevant information, and synthesizing their findings and that this causes them to founder in college. Since September, Gabriel has been teaching students how to use I-Charts to help them formulate effective research questions and then use these questions to manage multiple texts. Thus, by the time students begin their January study on reading and writing literary criticism, they are comfortable with the I-Chart process.

Gabriel meets with each student and together they explore the student's areas of interest in American fiction and formulate an appropriate research question around the student's interests. In working with Maria, for instance, Gabriel learned that she loved *Huckleberry Finn* but hated the ending. When Maria found out that there was a great deal of criticism on the issue of *Huckleberry Finn*'s ending, she got excited. After some revision, Maria developed this research question: Why is the ending of *Huckleberry Finn* so controversial?

Working with the school librarian, librarians at a local college, and Gabriel, Maria, like all the students, tracks down relevant sources and records essential information from each on her I-Chart (see Figure 5.2). As students conduct their reading, they keep track of repeating themes and central ideas that thread through the various texts as well as new ideas and questions that emerge during the research process. Students who have similar questions are encouraged to share resources as well as ideas.

Once the information has been recorded, students examine and discuss the way their own previous knowledge has been changed or solidified as a result of their research. After discussion, students develop a summary of their research and then work in Writers' Clubs to draft, receive feedback on, and revise their critical essays. Their final essays survey the range of critical ideas that exist on the topic and then develop an original critical perspective that draws on both the text and the literary criticism that surrounds it.

Figure 5.2. Maria's *Huckleberry Finn* I-Chart

Topic: Huckleberry Finn Question: Why is the ending of Huckleberry Finn so controversial?	
What do I already know? I know that there's critical disagreement about the ending. From my own perspective, the ending, especially the parts where Tom Sawyer creates a fake rescue for Jim, doesn't feel right. I kept waiting for Huck to put a stop to Tom's antics. I love the book, but hate the ending.	
Source 1 Lionel Trilling	Trilling thinks Huckleberry Finn is "an almost perfect work." He thinks the one flaw is the ending, where Tom sets up his series of escapes for Jim.
Source 2 T.S. Eliot	Eliot believes the ending is perfect. Brings reader back to mood of the beginning. It is neither happy nor tragic and leaves Huck as an outcast.
Source 3 Leo Marx	Marx thinks the ending is not in line with the characters of Huck and Jim and "jeopardizes the significance of the novel." Tom's antics rob Huck and Jim of the dignity they developed together. Also, Jim's freedom depends on a decision made by a slave owner—not realistic and dependent on all the things the novel is against.
Source 4 James Cox	Mostly agrees with Marx. Says the main reason for the discomfort of the ending is Tom Sawyer's return to the novel. Twain keeps pushing Huck into one more story, but that the final story doesn't work because it's Tom's story, not Huck's.
Source 5 Stephen Railton	Says there are two Jims—the Jim at the beginning and end, and the Jim in the middle. The one in the middle is a real and moral character, but the one at the end (and beginning) is a stereotype that appeals to whites' prejudices. It's unjust to return to this Jim at the end.
Summary	There is a *lot* of disagreement about this ending, but most of the critics seem to really hate the ending, like me. It seems that the critics who didn't like it think that the ending is not true to the characters of Huck and Jim. Another big reason is that the ending is racist because it turns Jim into a stereotype. Of those, I think that Marx's and Cox's positions are most like mine. I hadn't thought about the stereotyping issue much, but I really see it now.
Central ideas: Characterization Romanticism Realism Morality Racism	New questions to look into: Would surveying the class's opinions make this report more interesting?

Why the Strategy Works (What the Research Says)

As their name suggests, Inquiry Charts revolve around the use of questioning to search for information. Designed by Hoffman (1992) to move students beyond literal engagement with text and into the realm of critical thinking, the strategy makes use of three components that foster thinking beyond "the basics":

1. The strategy adapts Ogle's (1986) Know-Want-Learn (K-W-L) structure in which students form questions about the texts before reading and then use those questions to guide their inquiry and to determine how their knowledge has changed as a result.

2. The strategy accounts for different kinds of questions and encourages students to learn how to form their own critical-thinking questions. For example, one teacher's set of guidelines for helping students learn how to become good questioners follows:

   ■ Good critical-thinking questions result in longer answers.

   ■ Short-answer questions can be improved by following them with "Why?"

   ■ There are many different kinds of questions. Some ask for information, some ask the reader to reflect, and some ask for an evaluation or a prediction.

   ■ Try to include a variety of questions. (Not all I-Chart research focuses on a single question, as in Gabriel Booth's class. Often, students explore multiple questions using I-Charts; see Resources 5.1 and 5.2 for model I-Chart Organizers.)

3. The organizational structure of I-Charts is based on McKenzie's (1979) data charts, and it provides students with a systematic format for handling multiple texts and organizing information so that it is usable. I-Charts make the essential correlation between questioning and managing information, encourage students to consider how and why different texts on the same topic contain variations, and require students to keep track of sources and to record bibliographic information. For these reasons, the strategy naturally develops students' abilities as researchers and reporters.

Applications to Specific Content Areas

Common Question Patterns in Science, Math, Social Studies, and English/Language Arts

Figures 5.3, 5.4, 5.5, and 5.6, which follow shortly, summarize the most common types of questions asked in each of the four academic disciplines and provide examples of each type. These question patterns are taken from three main sources:

1. Textbooks from the various disciplines

2. State tests in the various disciplines (especially constructed-response questions)

3. Classroom questioning techniques used by teachers in various disciplines

Resource 5.1. I-Chart Organizer for a Single Research Question

Topic: Question:	
What do I already know?	
Source 1	
Source 2	
Source 3	
Source 4	
Source 5	
Summary	

Central ideas:	New questions to look into:

Resource 5.2. I-Chart Organizer for Multiple Questions

Topic	Question 1	Question 2	Question 3
What we think we know			
Source 1			
Source 2			
Source 3			
Source 4			
Summary			

Figure 5.3. Common Questions in Science

Question Type	Examples
Memory and Recall	• _____ motion of the planets occurs whenever the Earth passes or is passed by another planet. • Define *frequency, wavelength,* and *period.* • What adaptations allow bats to hunt at night?
Description	• Describe what happens during a solar eclipse.
Explanation	• Explain how an automobile's shock absorbers and springs keep the ride smooth.
Real-World Application	• How might a mechanic apply the scientific method to repair a car?
Cause and Effect (often, cause or effect)	• How was development of our scientific understanding of disease dependent on the invention of the microscope? • What are the causes of the current recurrence of tuberculosis?
Interpretation of Visual Data	• Examine this picture of a grizzly bear in its natural habitat. What visible characteristics help it to survive in this habitat? • The graph below shows the rates of conversion and amount of waste product generated by three different energy types. Which is the most efficient? Which is the most commonly used? How do you explain this difference? What conclusions can you draw from this information?
Compare and Contrast (often, compare or contrast)	• How do the parenting strategies of mammals differ from those of reptiles? How are they similar? • Coal and diamonds are both composed of carbon. What are the differences between the two forms?

Speculation and Hypothesis	• What changes in seismographic readings would lead scientists to believe the Earth's core was liquid instead of solid?
	• Two plants receive equal attention in a greenhouse, but one dies.
	  a. Develop a testable hypothesis to find out what happened.
	  b. Describe an experiment to test your hypothesis.
	  c. Describe results that would support your hypothesis.

The way to help students learn how to answer each of these important question types is through (we bet you already know this) modeling, in which the teacher thinks out loud to expose the thinking process behind the skill. Simply stated, we cannot expect students to be able to develop summaries or relate cause and effect if they have never seen and listened to someone who knows how to do these things well. After modeling, of course, students need practice and coaching as they learn to master the skills enlisted by various question types. The ideal way to handle question modeling throughout the year is through the strategy called QUESTing (Strong et al., 1995).

For example, using QUESTing to teach (or to remind) students how to answer questions that call for a summary might sound like this:

■ *Q*uestion all students.

How would you summarize Martin Luther King Jr.'s argument in "Letter From a Birmingham Jail"?

Figure 5.4. Common Questions in Math

Question Type	Examples
Drill and Practice	• Graph the following equations. • Solve for <u>x</u> below. • Find the volume of the conic sections below.
Definition and Description	• What is a common external tangent? • In your own words, explain the meanings of *mean, median,* and *mode.* • Describe an advantage of function notation.
Mathematical Expression	• Express the area <u>A</u> of a circle as a function of its circumference <u>C</u>.
Mathematical Explanation and Justification	• How does the size of angle A change as the measure of A goes from 10° to 80°? • Decide whether each ordered pair (a, b, and c, below) is a solution of: $$(x + y) \leq 3$$ $$(x - y) > 0$$ $$y \geq -3$$ Justify your answers graphically and algebraically. a. (3, 4) b. (1, –1) c. (–1, 3) • Would it be possible to write a system of linear inequalities whose graph is one of the stars in the American flag? Explain.
Generating Solutions	• Give two examples of equations that are not quadratic but can be expressed in quadratic form. • Find four solutions for $y = -x + \frac{3}{4}$ if $x = -1, 0, 1,$ and 2.
Analyzing Visual and Mathematical Data	• The box and whisker plot and bar graph below show the same information. Compare the two visual models in terms of how they convey data. • The line graph below shows the correlation between dog years and human years. a. What is the dog age of a one-year-old human? b. What is the human age of an eighteen-year-old dog? c. Write an equation to express the correspondence between dog and human years.
Creative Math	• Create a tessellating design of everyday shapes using a grid of rhombuses and using rotations and reflections.
Word Problems and Real-World Applications	• A 6′ 0″ man wants to know the height of his maple tree. He walks along the tree's shadow until his head is in a position where the end of his shadow exactly overlaps the end of the treetop's shadow. This puts him 9′ 6″ from the foot of the tree and 9′ 0″ from the end of the shadows. How tall is the maple? • Active Hardware is preparing to merge with Fleet House and Hardware. Active's profit can be expressed as 50x – 100. Fleet's profit can be expressed as 50x + 100. The two companies have decided to merge when their profits are the same. When will that occur? Explain your answer and your mathematical reasoning.

- *U*nderstand and model the thinking.

    OK, so what is this question asking for? Well, it's asking us to summarize King's argument. Now remember, when we summarize, what are we doing? We're creating a condensed restatement of the main points. So we have to be careful that we capture all the big ideas and essential

Figure 5.5. Common Questions in Social Studies

Question Type	Examples
Memory and Recall	• What is the policy of détente? • What physical features surrounding Mongolia made expansion difficult?
• Cause and Effect (Often cause or effect) • Relating Past to Present	• Describe the effect that the transformation of the U.S. from a rural to an industrial nation has had on different groups of Americans. • How did the fall of the Gupta Empire eventually lead to India's conquest? • How is the concept of balance of power used today?

Map Skills and Visual Analysis (maps, cartoons, charts, graphs, pictures)	• Based on this map showing territorial changes in Europe during the 1930s, which nations seem to have the greatest strategic value to the Axis powers? Why? Which nation appears to be in the most vulnerable position? Why?
	• This is a photo of a samurai noble
	  a. How would you describe the dress, shoes, sword, and hairstyle of the samurai?
	  b. What might make it difficult for the samurai to modernize his lifestyle?
	• Based on the graph
	  a. Which were the three largest and three smallest ethnic groups in 1775?
	  b. What general statements can you make about the ethnic composition of colonial America?

Interpreting Primary Documents	• Based on Kennedy's inaugural speech, how would you characterize Kennedy's style of foreign policy? How closely did he follow the premises outlined in the address? Is this address still the basis for current policy?
Compare and Contrast (often compare or contrast)	• Compare the aims and methods of the civil rights movement in the early 1960s with those of the late 1960s. • How was the influence of Chinese culture different in Japan than in Vietnam and Korea?
Developing a Position	• Was Oliver Cromwell a military dictator? Give examples to support your opinion. • Some Europeans were afraid that Charles V would establish a universal monarchy. Do you think it's possible for one person or government to gain complete control over Europe today? Why or why not?
Summarizing and Describing	• Summarize the military campaigns of Peter the Great. • Describe the actions taken by FDR in getting key economic policies passed and publicly supported.
Explaining and Interpreting	• Why did a tradition of independence and self-reliance develop in the back country? • How did the Mongols' ability to adapt to the environment help them expand?

details and that we leave out whatever information is not closely connected to those big ideas—that's how we summarize.

■ _E_stablish a gap between asking and answering.

Remember, this is not as simple as giving a yes-or-no type of answer. Take some time to think about what you need to do before you answer.

Figure 5.6. Common Questions in English/Language Arts

Question Type	Examples
Recall and Comprehension Check	• What are Kreton's reasons for coming to earth? • What do John and the girls see on their holiday? Whom do they meet?
Summary and Theme Finding	• State the theme and the larger point about life that the story makes. • How do the interactions among the characters help express the theme? • What impact does mother's decision to stand up for herself have on the family?
Explanation	• How does "The Cask of Amontillado" illustrate Poe's theory of the well-made tale? • Isolate and explain the purpose of the symbols used in the poem.
Literary Interpretation	• Why does Jody's attitude toward Grandpa change? • What is the author's purpose in writing this poem? • What does the narrator mean when he says "How easy it is to be strong in this world!"?
Compare and Contrast	• Compare and contrast the way Biff and Happy treat Willy in Act I. What do their interactions with their father reveal about their characters?
Opinion	• Do you think Swift goes too far in this essay? Why or why not?
Empathy	• Whose side would you take in this argument? Why?
Text-Specific Literary Elements	• Describe the tone and mood of this story. • What is ironic about the ending of "An Occurrence at Owl Creek Bridge"? How does point of view help to develop the irony? • Define allegory. How is *Pilgrim's Progress* an example of allegorical literature?

■ *S*earch for answers in notes or pictures.

Jot down notes, pictures, and ideas in your *Learning Logs*.

■ *T*alk in small groups.

Share your summaries with a neighbor. See if you can make some suggestions to each other about how to develop an ever better summary.

Strategies for Struggling Readers

Questions and questioning present three basic difficulties for struggling students:

1. They may have trouble understanding the thinking required by the question. For students who have difficulty understanding the thinking behind the question, use a study diet of modeling, QUESTing, and review of the common question types and the thinking they require (see the common question patterns in science, math, social studies, and English/language arts given earlier). Or you might teach

Figure 5.7. Question Menu

Reading the lines	**Reacting to the lines**
In which states did the Cherokee Indians live?	How would you feel if the government made your family move from your hometown?
Reading between the lines	**Reading beyond the lines**
Why do you think Sequoyah believed a written language would help his people return their culture?	Would a modern judge deem the 1830 Removal Act unconstitutional? Explain your answer.

students how to analyze questions to determine if a question is asking them to read the lines (find literal information), read between the lines (construct a response or make an inference), read beyond the lines (go outside the text to develop an answer), or react to the lines (explore their feelings and values). For example, Michael Ko regularly develops question menus like the one shown in Figure 5.7, allowing students to practice answering each type of question.

2. *They may have trouble extracting relevant information from a text or multiple texts.* The second difficulty students face is in pulling out relevant information from the texts they read, a problem discussed over and over again in this book. To facilitate active reading, a host of strategies are helpful, including Graphic Organizers, Questioning the Author, Reading for Meaning, and Compare and Contrast. Beyond the use and modeling of strategies, some useful suggestions include

- *Read Aloud sessions:* After students have read and internalized the questions and determined what they already know, read the text aloud and have them listen to it and form images from the words in their minds. Then, have students read it on their own.

- *Collaborative Reading:* Allow struggling students to work together. Each student may be responsible for finding answers to one question rather than three or four.

- *Reader's Punctuation:* Providing students with a shorthand technique (e.g., + answers my question, ~ conflicts with another source, – conflicts with my prior knowledge) can help the process by enabling students to remember the essential information in the texts they read.

Figure 5.8. Rubric for Developing Research Questions

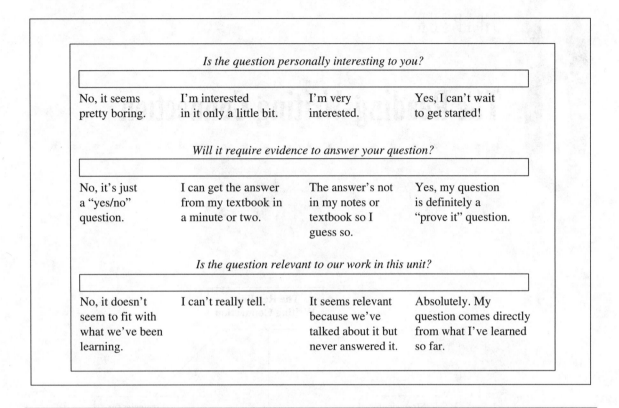

Is the question personally interesting to you?

| No, it seems pretty boring. | I'm interested in it only a little bit. | I'm very interested. | Yes, I can't wait to get started! |

Will it require evidence to answer your question?

| No, it's just a "yes/no" question. | I can get the answer from my textbook in a minute or two. | The answer's not in my notes or textbook so I guess so. | Yes, my question is definitely a "prove it" question. |

Is the question relevant to our work in this unit?

| No, it doesn't seem to fit with what we've been learning. | I can't really tell. | It seems relevant because we've talked about it but never answered it. | Absolutely. My question comes directly from what I've learned so far. |

3. They may have trouble generating their own questions. For students who have trouble generating questions about a topic, providing them with clear guidelines or a questioning rubric is especially helpful. For instance, Sue Marshton developed a simple, student-friendly rubric to help her eighth graders develop research questions for their I-Charts (see Figure 5.8). As students developed their questions, they referred to this rubric. During the process, Sue met with her students to help them develop better questions based on the rubric.

Teacher conferences and whole-class discussion can also facilitate question formulation for students. Sometimes, getting students to ask good questions is just a matter of probing their ideas by asking them to go beyond the facts and to ask "Why?" for the reasons behind the facts. For instance, a student might already know that earthquakes happen at cracks in the earth's surface; as a result, the student might not believe he or she has a question about this topic. Basic probing questions, such as "It's true that earthquakes happen at cracks in the earth, but why are these cracks there in the first place?" or "Do you know where these cracks are?" or "Yes, but what causes the cracks to push together?" help students see the countless questions that lie beneath the surface of any content.

CHAPTER

6

The Reading-Writing Connection

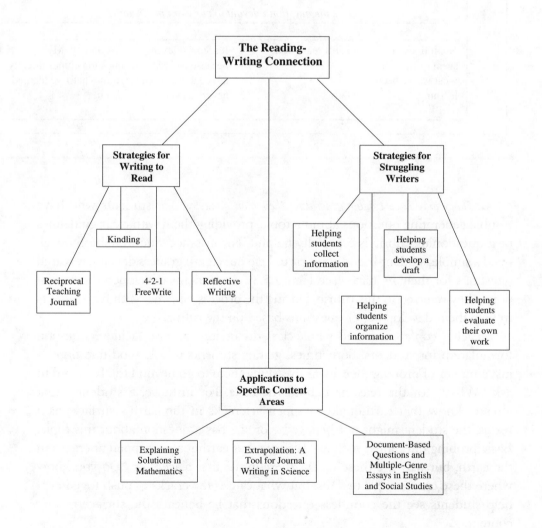

The Reading-Writing Connection

Strategies for Writing to Read

Kindling

Reciprocal Teaching Journal

4-2-1 FreeWrite

Reflective Writing

Strategies for Struggling Writers

Helping students collect information

Helping students develop a draft

Helping students organize information

Helping students evaluate their own work

Applications to Specific Content Areas

Explaining Solutions in Mathematics

Extrapolation: A Tool for Journal Writing in Science

Document-Based Questions and Multiple-Genre Essays in English and Social Studies

The Power of Writing About Reading

In our workshops, we often ask teachers this question: How does writing improve student reading? Here are some of the answers we've gotten back over the years:

> Writing and reading are like flip sides of the same coin. When students write, they get better at reading because they learn how to read their own work critically.

> Writing helps students think back on their reading—it helps them determine what was most important.

> It helps students connect what's in a reading to their own lives and experiences.

> When students write, they think like writers. This helps them as readers of other writers' work. It's a little like building a house—if you've never done it yourself, you can't very well critique or analyze another builder's work. But if you have experience in building a house, you know what to look for and how to evaluate what you see.

> They get better at seeing how texts are put together and how they work.

> After reading, we're full of ideas and questions. But when we write, we start to give shape to our ideas, to find an angle or perspective that helps us organize this information in a way that's meaningful to us.

We might condense and summarize these insights into five specific reasons why writing improves reading as follows:

1. Writing involves reading what we've written and asking questions about its strengths.

2. Writing about reading naturally makes us more reflective as we work to determine essential information and connect what we read to our lives.

3. Writing leads us through the same process that writers go through in creating the texts we read.

4. Writing gives us a deep, hands-on perspective on structure and technique as we work both consciously and unconsciously to produce more reader-friendly texts.

5. Writing helps us organize our responses to reading.

How to Make Student Journals Come to Life

In most classrooms, informal writing—writing that is more concerned with processing ideas and organizing thinking than with the production of a polished piece—tends to take one of two forms. Sometimes, teachers ask students to write either during a lesson or at home, to facilitate processing. Other times, informal writing is embedded into curriculum as part of an ongoing journal. We believe that all informal writing—whether embedded into curriculum or used spontaneously to deepen engagement—should be maintained in student journals for one very important reason: Journals provide a structure that allows students to look back over their work, select pieces for revision, and chart their own growth as readers, writers, and thinkers.

Yet our own experiences in the classroom may tell us that journals don't always work. For instance, it is not uncommon to find student journals where the writing produced in May shows little improvement over the writing from September. How do we make sure that journals are the powerful learning tools we know they can be? Our work with thousands of teachers across the country has taught us that there are five key ways to make journals come to life in the classroom:

1. Modeling: The best way to help students learn how to engage in thoughtful journal writing is to keep one yourself. Write about your experiences as a teacher, reader, parent, cook, golfer. Show students model entries from your journal. Talk about how you go about the process of keeping a journal. Think aloud to show them your thinking process in creating an entry.

2. Criteria: Students should regularly select a journal entry as the basis for more formal written work. In making a selection and working to expand and revise it, students need to be able to evaluate their own work according to clear criteria (e.g., Is it organized in a way that makes sense to the reader? Does it use the academic vocabulary of the subject area?). Criteria can be provided to students or developed with students through modeling and analyzing samples.

3. Feedback: Far more important than grading is feedback. Give students a grade, and that's the end of the process; there is little reason or encouragement to expand, refine, or explore further. But give them constructive, criteria-based suggestions on how they might improve, or provoke them to deepen their thinking through questions, and a different dynamic emerges—one that's in keeping with the cyclical nature of the writing process. For this reason, students should receive at least one or two personal responses to their writing every other week. To make this manageable, you might have students label every fifth page "Feedback."

4. Blending choice and assigned entries: Good classroom journal writing does not begin with statements like this: "Write about whatever you want." Instead, you should strive to develop a structure that encourages *controlled freedom.* Controlled freedom means that the student is not constrained by overly specific assignments (e.g., What powers does the executive branch hold?) but that the freedom students have to explore ideas is tied to essential learning and themes. By blending provocative, open-ended journal assignments (e.g., Why do you think people claim that Shakespeare is the ultimate universal writer?) with choice-based question menus that provide students with options about how best to respond, you can create a perfect balance between freedom and focus.

5. Samples: Experts in all the disciplines use journals. Bring in samples of journal writing from masters like Picasso, Thoreau, Darwin, Poincaré, and Churchill. Allow students to discover and discuss what makes for great journal writing.

We might think of these five ways of keeping journal writing alive as metastrategies, general strategies for journal writing. In the section that follows, we present four specific instructional strategies for writing about reading:

- *Reciprocal Teaching Journal* builds students' summarizing skills by applying the four proficient-reading techniques of Reciprocal Teaching (asking questions, managing new vocabulary, predicting, and summarizing) to a journal format.

- *Kindling* uses peer collaboration to help students generate and shape their initial responses to provocative questions and cues about essential content.

- *4-2-1 Free Write* allows students to negotiate with other students to discover the central idea in a reading and then to use a free-writing technique to explore that idea deeply.

- *Reflective Writing* taps into the power of metacognition to bring students closer to the processes of writing and reading.

We will also explore specific applications of writing about reading in relationship to the four major subject areas and provide a set of strategic interventions teachers can make for students who are stalled in different stages of the writing process.

Strategies for Writing to Read

Reciprocal Teaching Journal

Overview

Students naturally and spontaneously generate personal responses to (and questions about) the ideas, concepts, words, and facts they encounter during reading. The Reciprocal Teaching Journal provides students with a writing tool for expressing and organizing these responses by practicing the skills proficient readers use to deal with difficult texts: asking questions, managing new vocabulary, summarizing, and predicting.

Steps in Implementation

1. Select a challenging text for students to read.

2. Have students divide a page in their journals into two columns. On the left side, they record passages from the text they find confusing, challenging, or interesting. On the right, they pose questions, define unfamiliar vocabulary, and make predictions about events, arguments, or problems in the text.

3. After they have read the text and taken notes in their journals, ask students to form small groups to share their thoughts and attempt to answer any lingering questions about the reading.

4. Direct students to create a collaborative summary in their groups.

Strategy in the Classroom

In her ninth-grade World History class, Nancy Malloy has been using Reciprocal Teaching Journals with her students for several months now to dissect difficult texts. Today, they will be reading a text on Ancient Egypt during the New Kingdom.

As Nancy hands out the reading, her students open their journals and divide a page into two columns: notes from text on the left; and questions (Q), vocabulary (V), and predictions (P) on the right (Figure 6.1 shows an example of such a page). While her students read and write, Nancy circulates throughout the room to monitor student progress and help those who may be having difficulty.

When the students have completed their reading and writing, they form small groups to share ideas and help one another answer questions that emerged during their reading. Once each group feels as though they have a firm understanding of the text, Nancy asks each group to write a collaborative summary. She points students to the four criteria she has listed on the board for writing a good summary.

Your summary should

1. Cover the key points of the text

2. Answer the question(s) your group considered

3. Include new vocabulary you encountered

4. Make a prediction about the next period in Egyptian history

Figure 6.1. Student Example–Ancient Egypt

Notes from text	Questions (Q), vocabulary (V), predictions (P)	
Female pharaoh Hatshepsut organized trading expeditions to the land of Punt, south of the Red Sea.	Who were the inhabitants of the land of Punt? What was so special about trading with them?	Q
Thutmossides were keen on establishing foreign domination.	Is this a reaction to the Hyksos invasions of earlier periods?	Q
Akhenaten promoted monotheism by declaring Aten the one and only God.	Monotheism: the belief that there is only one God. I don't think this belief lasted very long because the Greeks and Romans believed in many gods, and they came after the Egyptians.	V P
Akhenaten was often portrayed androgynously in sculpture.	Androgynous: having both male and female characteristics. How can historians be sure this wasn't just how he actually looked?	V Q

Why the Strategy Works (What the Research Says)

In developing the strategy known as Reciprocal Teaching, Palinscar and Brown (1984) identified four skills or reading strategies used by proficient readers:

1. *Asking questions* helps focus attention and allows proficient readers to actively engage the text.

2. *Managing new vocabulary* means clarifying concepts or unfamiliar words students encounter during reading.

3. *Summarizing* allows proficient readers to check their understanding of a text periodically by condensing specific facts and details into a general summary.

4. *Predicting* refers to the active speculation about what will follow in a given reading.

The Reciprocal Teaching Journal puts these strategies into action through writing, thereby enabling students to shape and clarify the "inner conversations, which they use to discover what they know" (Silver et al., 1996, p. 227). Furthermore, Tierney and Shanahan (1991) and Vacca and Vacca (1998) confirm what many teachers have known for years: The more that students practice writing, the clearer their thinking becomes about both reading and writing.

Making the strategy even more powerful is its Cooperative Learning component, which implements the five essential elements of group learning that foster student confidence with difficult texts (Johnson & Johnson, 1999):

1. Positive interdependence: The group must understand the text together. If one student doesn't understand, then the group does not understand.

2. Face-to-face interaction: Sharing questions and ideas and helping each other through difficulties provides positive reinforcement.

3. Individual and group accountability: Each student must share and contribute ideas about the text for the group to function.

4. Interpersonal and small group skills: Students increase their competence in communicating ideas, respecting others' interpretations, resolving conflicts, and summarizing ideas.

5. Group processing: Reflecting on all ideas and key points in the reading allows students to pool and then shape their ideas into a collaborative summary.

Kindling

Overview

Personal thoughts, ideas, arguments, or questions we have about the texts we read are sometimes difficult to organize or explain clearly. This is especially true for students who are asked to read, absorb, and generate ideas in a variety of content areas.

The Kindling strategy, developed by Silver et al. (1996), uses provocative questions that help students generate informal ideas and activate prior knowledge. These ideas are then fleshed out through writing and peer collaboration to become the foundation for active reading. Kindling can also be used as a postreading strategy in which students explore the meaning of a reading, discuss their ideas, and generate initial written responses.

Steps in Implementation

1. Before students read a text or texts, pose an open-ended or provocative question about the topic.

2. Encourage students to take time to consider what they need to know to answer the question and how what they already know might help their understanding.

3. Refer students to their journals to sketch their thoughts using whole sentences, short notes, or even images.

4. Once ideas have been generated and recorded, have students meet with their peers in pairs or small groups. The goal is for students to

   ■ Look for similarities or differences in their writing

   ■ Summarize their ideas

   ■ Generate additional ideas and questions

5. Record students' ideas on a chart paper or chalkboard, and discuss.

6. Have students read the given text, using their journals to guide the process.

Strategy in the Classroom

Kara Pickett is using the Kindling strategy to open a unit on the human circulatory system with her tenth-grade biology class. She is going to have her students read a text explaining Starling's hypothesis, which solved the problem of how blood transports nutrients and gets rid of waste. But first, Kara seeks to kindle her students' interest. She begins,

> I want you all to imagine a train pulling a bunch of cars that are filled to capacity with cargo. The train is traveling on a web of intertwining tracks, and all the tracks are inside tunnels. Does everyone have the image in their heads? OK, now I want you to take out your journals and write some thoughts on this question: How is our circulatory system like that train?

Kara's students open their journals, and she has them divide a page into two columns. On one side of the page, the students record what they already know about the circulatory system that will help them answer the question (e.g., blood vessels carry oxygen, water, and other nutrients). On the other side, they record what they need to know to answer the question more completely (e.g., how do blood vessels get rid of the nutrients they carry?).

After the students have had time to jot down some ideas, Kara asks them to form groups of two or three. In their groups, students share their ideas and examine them with critical yet considerate eyes. They spend some time merging their thoughts and noting any new questions that arise in the process before coming together as a class for discussion. During the discussion, ideas are shared freely and students seek resolution on any lingering questions.

Next, Kara and her students explore how writing before reading helps them build their knowledge base while she records students' thoughts on the board. She then works with students to organize scattered thoughts and identify gaps in their prereading knowledge so they know what to look for as they read. Kara reminds students to slow their minds down and to use their journals to guide their reading.

Why the Strategy Works (What the Research Says)

The Kindling strategy, adapted from Silver et al. (1996), helps students put their own best prereading ideas into writing. This writing then serves as a framework for careful reading, as students add, refine, and revise their understanding in light of the text. The strategy is particularly effective for four reasons:

1. Because so much research points to the importance of activating prior knowledge, Kindling uses provocative questions and reflective thinking and writing to help students tap into their memory banks and pull out what they already know about the topic.

2. The journal-writing component enables students to organize what they know and to retain what they generate during their prereading thinking.

3. The wiring in of peer and group discussion gives students a chance to test out, revise, and synthesize their ideas before discussion and reading.

4. The strategy takes a constructivist, quest-oriented approach to learning and reading, allowing students to make original connections, transform their ideas, and "follow trails of interest" that lead to independent learning (Brooks & Brooks, 1999, p. 22).

There are a variety of formats for Kindling. The CREATE IDEAS chart shown in Figure 6.2 provides a number of writing frames that will get students started, help you meet specific objectives, and develop particular thinking skills. We suggest you rotate frames throughout the year but that you focus on specific skills long enough to help students make progress.

4-2-1 Free Write

Overview

Often, students have a hard time thinking through or even determining the central idea that holds a reading or set of readings together. By working collaboratively to identify "the one big idea" and then exploring that idea through free writing, students develop a deep and personally resonant perspective on how texts convey their most essential information.

Figure 6.2. CREATE IDEAS Chart

C	Compare & Contrast	*To determine differences or similarities on the basis of certain criteria:* • List similarities and differences. • Compare and contrast the following _____. • What are the significant similarities or differences between _____ and _____? • What two are most similar or most different?
R	Relate Personally	*To describe one's emotional state or feeling or how one would apply what was learned to some part of his or her own life:* • What are your feelings about _____? • How would you feel if _____ happened to you? • What would you do if _____ happened to you? • What are some possible feelings you had when that happened?
E	Evaluate	*To appraise the value or worth of a thing or idea or to make a quantitative or qualitative judgment concerning specific criteria:* • Which alternative would you choose and why? • What are the advantages or disadvantages of _____? • Given the following choices, justify or substantiate your selection.
A	Associate	*To relate objects/thoughts as they come to mind:* • Free, controlled, or linked association. • What words/ideas come to mind when I say _____? • What do you think of when you listen to the _____? • What do you think of when you see the _____?
T	Trace/ Sequence	*To arrange information in a logical order according to chronology, quantity, quality, or location:* • Trace the development of _____. • Sequence the events leading up to _____. • What do you do first when you _____?
E	Enumerate	*To list in concise form or to name one after another:* • List the causes of the _____. • List the facts regarding _____. • List the steps involved in _____.
I	Identify & Describe	*To identify the properties of particular items, happenings, or concepts:* • What did you see, hear, note? • Describe the facts. • What did you observe? • Describe the characteristics or properties of the object.
D	Define	*To give the meaning of a word or concept:* • Define the following concept. • Define what is meant by _____. • Define the word from the context clues.
E	Explore & Predict	*To generate alternatives and assumptions concerning cause and effect:* • How many ways can you _____? • What would happen if _____? • Suppose _____ happened? What would be the consequences?

(continued)

Figure 6.2. Continued

A	**Argue a Position**	*To explain good reasons for a particular position; to present facts to support your position:* • Where do you stand on this issue? • Justify your position. • Explain your argument. • What are your reasons for taking this position?
S	**Summarize**	*To state briefly or in conclusive form the substance of what has been observed, heard, or experienced:* • Summarize what you read. • Think of a title for the story. • Draw a picture that summarizes what you learned. • The point of view of the lecture was _____.

SOURCE: Adapted from Silver et al. (2001).

Steps in Implementation

1. After students have read a text or set of texts, ask them to write the four big ideas on their 4-2-1 Free Write Organizer (see Resource 6.1).

2. Have students pair up to share their ideas and to select the two most important ideas from their lists.

3. Allow student pairs to meet with another pair, share their two ideas, and reach agreement on the single most important idea.

4. Collect and discuss the most important idea from each group. Together, select the idea that is the most important.

5. Instruct students to write freely for five minutes on the selected idea, explaining what they know about the idea so that someone who was not in the class would understand it. Students must write without stopping; if they get stuck, they should write about why they are stuck.

6. Ask students to return to their groups of four to listen to each other's written responses.

7. Hold a discussion on the big idea and look for ways to link students' new understanding to the next topic or unit. Have students select one piece of free writing each month for further development.

Strategy in the Classroom

Andrea del Rio knows the value of free writing in her geometry class. She says,

Too often, math classrooms run through so many concepts so quickly that students never get the chance to internalize and personalize the biggest concepts under which so many smaller ones fit—essential concepts like the relationship between geometry and space that really drive the discipline. You can't just treat concepts like these as if they're isolated from all the subconcepts beneath them. Otherwise, students can never see their way to the big picture. That's why I like to use short, conceptual readings like the texts in *Investigating Mathematics: The Touchstones Approach* [Zeiderman, 1994] in my classroom and to have students come to terms with these enormous concepts through free writing.

It is the first week of school, and Andrea's students are busy reading one of the texts from *Investigating Mathematics* (Zeiderman, 1994) called "Foundations of Geometry" by the German mathematician David Hilbert. In this excerpt, Hilbert explains how the whole of geometry rests on only a few simple axioms and discusses the crucial axioms of connection and order. Once students have completed the reading, Andrea asks each student to list four central ideas. Then, students pair up, and the two partners must distill their ideas by agreeing on the two most important ideas. Last, students pair up again, creating groups of four, to negotiate their ideas and determine the single most important idea in the text.

Andrea says,

It's always instructive to hear them negotiating their ideas. You really get a chance to see how their minds work—how they interact, think, and express themselves. After they're done negotiating, we talk about each group's ideas, focusing on how they justified their decision and looking for both the connections and disparities between different groups' ideas. Then, we reach our final consensus. As a class, we decide which group's idea best captures the essential message of the text, and once they have that, they use it as the conceptual foundation for their free writing.

Students write about the chosen idea for five minutes without stopping. If they get stuck, Andrea reminds them that they should write about *why* they are stuck—about what in the content or the process seems to be holding their pens back. When five minutes are up, students reconvene with their groups of four and read what they wrote to their fellow group members. Students are not to judge each other's work; rather, they are to listen and to note where the thinking seemed strongest and where the ideas seemed to lag. Because students select one piece of informal writing each month to develop into more formal writing, the idea is to help each student see how the ideas contained in the free writing might be made more powerful.

Andrea goes on to say,

After this is all done—the negotiation of ideas, the free writing, the reading aloud—students have a great foundation for future learning. We've laid a great base, and now we're ready to start adding the floors, the windows, and the decoration.

Why the Strategy Works (What the Research Says)

There is a significant body of research pointing to the value and effectiveness of free writing in all classrooms. Some of the findings are the following:

- Free writing increases comfort and decreases the self-consciousness many students associate with writing (Veit, 1981).

- Free writing makes it clear that writing is a *process*, not a final product (Veit, 1981).

- Free writing, especially in conjunction with a prewriting prompt, helps students move from writing at the sentence level to writing at the text level (Knudson, 1989).

- Free writing and writing feedback focused on meaning and ideas rather than error correction improves students' overall writing quality (Song, 1998).

- Free writing that includes talking and discussion as part of the process creates the kind of communication-rich environment that fosters experimentation and confidence (Reid, 1983).

- Free writing about particular texts increases reading comprehension (Williams, 1992).

These benefits being said, however, a common criticism of free writing is that it is so unstructured that charting growth and anchoring it to essential content can sometimes be difficult. 4-2-1 Free Write is designed specifically to capitalize on the great benefits of free writing while minimizing its potential pitfalls. By making use of paired and group negotiation processes folded between class discussions on the essential idea of a text or set of texts, the strategy keeps students rooted firmly to the content. The inclusion of postwriting feedback groups helps students to see how they might improve both their writing and their comprehension without the pressure of judgment. And last, by asking students to select one of their free writes to develop into a more formal monthly product, 4-2-1 Free Write reiterates the process-oriented nature of writing and helps both teacher and student see the progress the student is making in mastering this process.

Reflective Writing

Overview

Have you ever called a specific memory to mind to think about it in greater detail? All of us do this regularly and when we do, we deepen the memory in terms of our comprehension of it and our connection to it. In a similar way,

Resource 6.1. 4-2-1 Free Write Organizer

4-2-1 Free Write Organizer

Individually: Four Ideas

Pairs: Two Central Ideas

Groups of Four: The One Big Idea

Free Write (Use the back of this sheet or a new piece of paper for more space.)

Reflective Writing provides students with the opportunity to reflect in writing so that they develop a long-lasting and personally relevant perspective on the texts they read.

Steps in Implementation

1. Provide students with a reading on a given topic.

2. Ask students to stop after they have read the first two or three key ideas in the reading. Frame reflective questions for students to ponder. (Be sure to include questions about the content and about the reading process.)

3. Have students organize their thoughts and record them in their journals.

4. Direct students to form small groups to match, share, and compare their thoughts with others.

5. Engage students in an activity that encourages them to summarize and synthesize what they have learned.

6. Encourage students to develop reflective questions on their own, as a way to gain greater perspective on the content and process of reading.

Strategy in the Classroom

Andrea Holt knows how difficult it can be for students to read and understand scientific technical writing. "The structure and content of technical writing is so different from what they read in other subjects," says Andrea, "which makes it hard to pick out the essential information."

Today, Andrea presents her chemistry students with a research article on snowmobile emissions in Yellowstone National Park from the *Journal of Environmental Science and Technology.* She asks them to read only the abstract and the introduction to the article before stopping to think about the following questions:

- What are the two most important ideas so far?

- How do the researchers intend to use the data they've collected? And is their data reliable?

- Did you have any trouble understanding particular passages? Which ones? Why?

- How do you think this research relates to what we studied yesterday?

Students take time to organize their thoughts and begin to record them in their journals.

Andrea then has her students form small groups to share and compare thoughts. She explains,

As you examine what you've written and your reflections, read your writing slowly, paying attention to your own inner voice. In your groups, I want you to pool your answers to the questions into a brief summary of what you've read so far, noting what you found difficult and why. Your journal writing and summarizing will give you a sense of what some technical writers go through as they write. Understanding the process of writing can sometimes make it easier to read what others have written.

When they have finished their brief summaries, Andrea's students continue reading the research study, pausing every few sections to engage in reflective writing. Within a few weeks, students are comfortable enough with the strategy to actively reflect while reading on their own.

Why the Strategy Works (What the Research Says)

It is not uncommon for students to become bored and unmotivated when faced with difficult reading. The reasons for this are numerous, but the most common are a lack of active personal engagement with the text and no method for working through difficulties. Reflective Writing helps students overcome these problems by encouraging them to reflect on and write about their growing understanding of the content of the reading and on their own reading process.

Research conducted by Brown (1989) and Marzano et al. (1988) emphasizes the importance of metacognitive thinking for stimulating student motivation and learning. When students are asked to think about their own thinking, they learn to be more self-regulated in their learning and begin to see what kinds of thinking come naturally to them and what kinds pose difficulties. By using writing to record this metacognition, students overtly expose their thinking processes as they read. Thus, discussions about improvement are more productive and effective.

Applications to Specific Content Areas

Explaining Solutions in Mathematics

Nowhere is the connection between reading, thinking, and writing in mathematics more evident than in the increasing number of state tests now asking students to explain the reasoning they use to solve word problems. What the makers of these tests have come to realize is that the thinking behind the solution is as important as the solution itself. Writing, with its power to make cognitive processes overt, is the perfect tool for helping students clarify and succinctly explain their problem-solving processes.

Explaining Solutions moves through five steps:

1. Assign students a word problem to solve in class. Students read the problem carefully and underline the question and the essential information.

2. Allow students to solve the problem. When they are finished, they should reflect on the process and list, in order, the steps they followed.

3. Work with students to use transitional words (e.g., *first, next, then, finally*) to convert steps into paragraph form. (Over time, students should become independent.)

4. Have students reread their explanations, and ask,

   ■ Does it include all the steps?

   ■ Do any terms need clarification?

   ■ Are the steps in the correct order?

   ■ Are the transitional words well chosen?

5. Encourage students to revise and refine their explanations as necessary.

Extrapolation: A Tool for Journal Writing in Science

How does it work? What are its parts? How is it put together? What writing techniques are particularly effective? Imagine how radically student writing would improve if, when students approached a text, they used such questions to figure out how authors write and then applied what they learned to their own writing. Writers of all types—literary, technical, scientific, journalistic—when stalled in the act of writing, revert to reading, searching for ideas and techniques that other writers have used to solve similar problems. This active search makes them better readers and writers. Extrapolation is a tool that helps students discover and apply the often hidden lessons of high-quality texts. In the science classroom, the strategy is especially beneficial in teaching students how to write in the different genres of the discipline—explanations, scientific arguments, even lab reports.

For example, Terrell Childs has spent much of the first two months of the year helping his seventh-grade earth science students learn to write scientific explanations and, more recently, arguments. By incorporating high-quality writing models from online scientific journals, Terrell has seen many students adopt the techniques of sophisticated writers. Today, he is working on helping students improve their arguments by learning how to foresee and respond to counterarguments.

"Now, I want you all to read this carefully," says Terrell, handing out an editorial from the local paper arguing against the placement of a landfill in the county, "and I want you to keep three questions in mind: What can we learn from the way this writer foresees counterarguments? What might others say against her position? And what can we learn from the way she responds?"

Students read the editorial individually, then meet in pairs to share their initial responses. Terrell then holds a class discussion to collect ideas and to help students back their ideas with textual evidence.

Terrell: So, who has an idea?

Sam: Well, for one thing, they talk to people.

Terrell: What do you mean? How do you know that?

Sam: Well, over here it says, "Some people are saying that a landfill's the best choice because it's the cleanest choice." So she must have spoken to some people about it.

Terrell: Good. Let's put that on our list: *To foresee counterarguments, good writers talk with others.*

Terrell continues until the class has generated and substantiated four ideas; then he has students work in groups of four to read their most recent arguments. Student groups listen to each member's piece and brainstorm possible counterarguments, as well as possible responses to the counterargument. If the student does not have the information needed to respond effectively, Terrell helps the student find an appropriate print or Internet resource. Students use the results of this brainstorming session to fend off possible attacks on their arguments as Terrell and the class add a new dimension to their rubrics for writing good arguments: *Good arguments foresee and respond to counterarguments.*

Document-Based Questions and Multiple-Genre Essays in English and Social Studies

The past five years have seen a rapid expansion of items on state tests asking students to read, interpret, and then write about a group of texts linked by theme or concept that they are seeing for the first time. Whereas these document-based and multiple-genre essays used to appear only on advanced-placement tests in History and English, we now see states that are requiring them as early as fifth grade. The question we have to ask ourselves is, How do we help students conduct the kind of reading that will make thoughtful writing possible?

Here is a five-step process (along with a running example) that you can model with students to help them succeed in crafting these demanding essays.

1. Analyze the question or test item for key words and topics. For example, one test gives students three texts: In the first, a Chinese student describes her first three months in an American school, the second describes a classroom during an air raid drill, and the last is a poem on teaching. Students are asked to discuss how these three texts contribute to their understanding of how teachers help students learn. Thus, the key topic is *how teachers help students learn.*

2. Generate what is already known about the topic. Once students have determined the central topic, they should create a concept map that contains everything they know about the topic.

3. Use this prior knowledge to actively search for examples in the text. With prior knowledge out in the open and organized, reading becomes focused and active. Students should annotate the texts as they read them, using underlining, arrows, margin notes, and the like to mark and contextualize the important information.

4. Move text annotations into the concept map. At this point, students should expand and revise their concept maps by putting the information from the texts into their original concept maps. This way, students have comprehensive maps that include their own ideas and the examples and ideas from the texts—exactly what they need in order to discuss how the texts contribute to their understanding of how teachers help students learn.

5. Lay out the sequence for writing. Thinking too early about the writing sequence interferes with students' thinking about their own prior knowledge and the information in the texts. Now that students have thought through and organized this foundational thinking, they are ready to lay out the sequence for the essay.

Strategies for Struggling Writers

Writing, whether formal or informal, is a process that includes

- Collecting information
- Organizing information
- Developing a draft or drafts
- Evaluating one's own work

When we assess students' written work, we can determine which of these skills—these essential phases in the writing process—require the most attention. Figure 6.3 outlines ways to determine which of these skills need attention and offers strategies that help students develop each skill.

Figure 6.3. Skill Outline

If the writing is …	The student may need help in …	Strategies that can help …
Complete, but minimal in terms of content	Collecting information	• *Brainstorming.* Student brainstorms all she knows about the topic and what she needs to learn to complete the task. Student reads, takes notes, separates main ideas from important details. • *Generating Questions.* Student generates a list of questions that will help the reader understand the topic, then reads and takes notes on which questions were answered and which still need answering. • *Visualizing.* Student visualizes, then draws ideas related to task and topic. Drawing becomes the basis for brainstorming. • *Peer Collection.* Student talks to a peer on what she knows/thinks she knows/needs to know. Peer takes notes that guide students through reading. Students re-pair to discuss what the writing will be like.
Digressive, often wandering off on tangents	Organizing information	• *Fat T's.* Student draws several fat T's: **T** In the top of the T she writes a main idea she wants to communicate. In the base, she lists supporting details. Student numbers Ts in order for writing. • *Grouping.* Student brainstorms all she might include in her writing, then places items that go together into groups. Student labels each group and decides on their order. • *Extrapolation.* Student finds a model similar to what she will write, analyzes structure and order, and develops an outline for her piece. Then she rereads the model for techniques the author used to keep the reader's interest and uses these ideas to guide her own writing. • *Peer Organization.* Student organizes notes into a beginning, middle, and end. She tells a friend about her piece and asks the friend to take notes and to help find out which parts were hard to understand.
Strong at the outset but weakens as it goes on	Drafting	• *Orderless Drafting.* Student labels three sheets of paper "beginning," "middle," and "end," then picks one sheet and drafts that part before moving to another sheet. It is not necessary to start at the beginning. If the student gets stuck, she should jump to another sheet. • *Question-Based Drafting.* Student brainstorms a list of questions the reader might want answered, and then writes to answer all the questions. Student converts each question into a good opening sentence for each paragraph. • *Freewriting.* Student forces herself to write without stopping for a set amount of time. If she gets stuck, she should close her eyes, imagine she is an idea, and write about herself. • *Drafting to the Letter.* Student pretends her piece is a letter to a friend and asks herself what her friend would want to hear. Then, they draft with the friend's interests in mind.

(continued)

Figure 6.3. Continued

| Inconsiderate of the reader (e.g., assumes key information is already known or spends too much time on obvious or unnecessary information) | Evaluating his/her own work | • *Clarifying Purpose.* Without looking at her piece, the student writes notes on what she meant to say in the beginning, middle, and end. Then she reads the piece, looking for places where she did not communicate what she meant to say and revising accordingly.
• *Critical Reading.* Student determines criteria for the kind of writing she has done (or gets a rubric from the teacher). She finds a similar piece and identifies its strengths and weaknesses using the criteria. Then she compares and contrasts it with her own piece, making notes for revision.
• *Imagining a Reader.* Student imagines what she wants her reader to feel or think about each section of her piece and makes notes on it. Then, she reads her piece to a friend, asks what the friend thinks and feels about each section, and makes notes. She uses her notes to develop a revision plan.
• *Reading Aloud.* Student has a partner read her own piece to her and makes notes on words, phrases, or sentences that sound clumsy. These notes become the basis for revision. |

Reading Styles

The Key to Reading Success

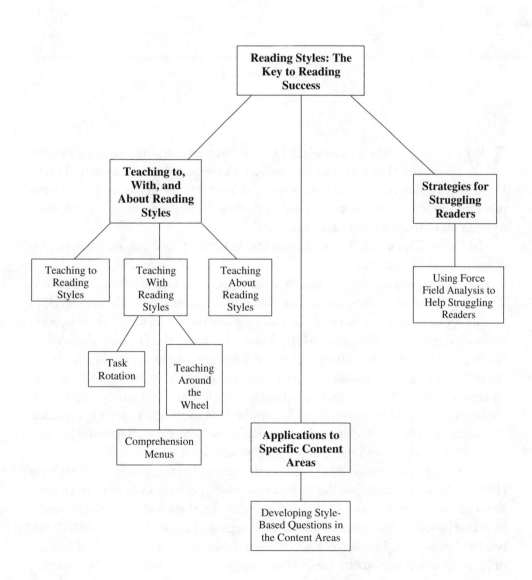

Figure 7.1. Mark and Teola

Mark	Teola
I like reading that teaches me how to do something, whether it's to set up my new computer or improve my game in tennis. But start talking about how a cell is like a factory or about this thing one of my English teachers calls "getting lost" in a book and reading becomes work for me. I try to stay focused on the facts and the useful information. A lot of my friends always complain about having to read their textbooks, but believe it or not, I actually like it. I'm really good at remembering the dates and names in history and the new vocabulary words when I read my science textbook.	Reading is like watching a movie in your head. I really love it when authors write so that you can actually see what they see or when they ask me to imagine what it's like to walk in someone else's shoes. I just finished the *Lord of the Rings* trilogy by J.R.R., Tolkien and I'm so sad it's over. Reading those books was like escaping into another world; I felt like Alice in Wonderland.

What are you like as a reader? Do you have any reading routines or idiosyncrasies? Do you read best in bed, in the park, at a desk, in a library? Do you read slowly, mulling over words, characters, and ideas as if they were precious gifts? Or do you read quickly, finding precisely what you need, then moving on to the next section of the text?

In Figure 7.1, two high school students, Mark and Teola, share their experiences as readers with us.

At a quick glance, we can see that there are profound differences between Teola and Mark as readers. Each is attracted to different kinds of texts—Mark to textbooks and Teola to fantasy. Even more significantly, Mark and Teola process textual information differently. Mark focuses on facts, details, and skills while reading but has trouble with metaphorical language and imagery. Teola, on the other hand, processes reading through her imagination by trying to "see" the cinematic quality of the characters, settings, and ideas she encounters. Last, each student has very different purposes for reading: Mark wants to turn his reading into something he can use or apply, whereas Teola savors the images she has created in her head. We call these differences *reading styles.*

Our reading style model is based on the groundbreaking work of Carl Jung (1923), who discovered that the way people take in information and make decisions about the importance of that information develops into personality types. It is also based on the work of Kathleen Briggs and Isabel Myers (1962/1998), who elaborated on Jung's work to develop a comprehensive model of human differences made famous by their Myers-Briggs Type Indicator®. By applying

Figure 7.2. Four Styles of Readers

Mastery-Style Readers ...	Interpersonal-Style Readers ...
Read because they want to learn practical information	*Read because* they want to understand themselves and other people
Like texts that are clear, to the point, and have useful applications	*Like texts that* focus on feelings, relationships, and human stories
Approach reading by looking over the text for its sections before reading, focusing on the details while reading, and remembering facts and details after reading	*Approach reading by* asking how the text is connected to their life before reading; focusing on their feelings during reading; and discussing the text's relevance to their life after reading
Like reading questions that ask them to recall information	*Like reading questions that* ask them how they feel or what they would do in a given situation
Experience difficulty when texts become too poetic or fantasy-oriented	*Experience difficulty when* texts become too abstract or complicated
Want a reading teacher who shows them what they need to know step by step	*Want a reading teacher who* leads exciting discussions on what the text means to them
Understanding-Style Readers ...	**Self-Expressive-Style Readers ...**
Read because they want to be challenged to think	*Read because* they want to use their imagination
Like texts that contain provocative ideas and controversial issues	*Like texts that* are poetic, fantasy-oriented, and stylistically creative
Approach reading by determining what questions they want the text to answer before reading; focusing on ideas and logic during reading; and asking questions after reading	*Approach reading by* making predictions before reading; focusing on images during reading; doing creative work after reading
Like reading questions that ask them to explain, prove, or take a position	*Like reading questions that* ask them to speculate, imagine, and ask "What if?"
Experience difficulty when texts focus too strongly on feelings	*Experience difficulty when* texts are too detail-oriented
Want a reading teacher who makes them think	*Want a reading teacher who* gives them interesting reading projects

this model to our own research on reading, we have been able to identify four distinct styles of readers, as shown in Figure 7.2.

Of course, no one has just one style. Reading styles are not fixed categories that make one person a Mastery reader and another an Interpersonal reader. Throughout our lives and in various situations, we use all four styles to solve the problems posed by various texts. But it is also true that most of us develop familiarity and strength in one or two styles, and we tend to be weaker in one or two other styles. This means that reading styles are the key to motivating students and helping them experience the joys of success. The trick is to help students capitalize on their strengths by accommodating their dominant styles while encouraging them to stretch and grow their capacities in their weak styles.

Why Are Reading Styles Important?

Because of our learning styles, different texts prove more difficult than others for us. Interpreting symbolism in Romantic poetry requires a different kind of thinking than learning the steps in solving polynomial equations from a textbook. Reading both texts in the same way will likely lead to a severely diminished understanding of at least one of the texts, whether it's by John Keats or the authors of *Algebra I*. Similarly, the processes involved in working to identify with the plight of the endangered panda will not be of much use when it comes to evaluating the logic behind an essay on the effectiveness of U.S. foreign policy during Vietnam. The different thinking processes involved in exploring symbols, learning new skills, identifying with content, and evaluating arguments enlist different reading styles, meaning that some types of reading will be more or less challenging for us, depending on our styles.

Making matters even more difficult, most texts operate on multiple levels at the same time. Students cannot simply read one text for its literal information, another for its imagery, a third for its emotional relevance, and a fourth for its logic. Think, for example, of a local newspaper editorial urging residents to vote yes on the school budget. Somewhere near the beginning of the editorial, we might expect to find the important factual information: the key players involved, when election day takes place, the proposed numbers, and so forth. Another part of the editorial might be more polemical—setting up arguments, tearing down counterarguments, and working to marshal evidence and draw logical conclusions. We might also find in this editorial a good deal of speculation, probably centered on predicting what would happen to the schools if the budget is rejected. Last, because good editorial writers know that a persuasive case should appeal personally and emotionally as well as logically to the reader, we would probably find an emotionally charged conclusion urging everyone to get out and vote yes.

We can see, by examining new state testing systems, the growing awareness of the fact that different texts make different demands on readers and that all texts need to be understood in multiple lights. In New York State, for example, the four overarching reading standards require that students be able to read for information (Mastery reading), for critical analysis and evaluation (Understanding reading), for literary response and expression (Self-Expressive reading), and for social interaction (Interpersonal reading).

In this chapter, we will explore three ways of putting the power of style to work in reading instruction:

- *Teaching to* students' styles, which means creating a support structure for struggling readers that validates and capitalizes on their strengths as readers

- *Teaching with* styles by differentiating instruction and assessment so that all students are both accommodated by working in their strong styles and challenged to grow by developing their weaker styles

Figure 7.3. Guidelines for Working With Mastery Readers

Start with clear expectations	1. State the purpose of the reading and demonstrate the importance of its content. 2. Demonstrate and model the skills needed to conduct the reading.
Tell students what they need to know and how to do it step-by-step	1. Establish what students already know about the content and help them tap into their prior knowledge. 2. Teach students how to break larger texts into more manageable segments. 3. When showing students how to apply a reading strategy, teach one step at a time and allow time for practice and coaching. 4. Encourage students to determine difficult vocabulary and to look up these terms before and during reading. 5. Move students from "getting the gist" to forming broader interpretations.
Establish opportunities for concrete experiences and for exercise and practice	1. Model and teach active note-making strategies such as Split-Screen Notes and Four-Way Reporting and Recording. 2. If possible, fold in hands-on materials and active processing activities (e.g., a model of a molecule, math exercises). 3. Teach students how to create and use graphic organizers. 4. Provide for directed, guided, and independent practice in key reading skills, especially those requiring internalization.
Provide speedy feedback on student performance	1. Regularly check for understanding. 2. Teach students how to look for gaps in their understanding. 3. Provide regular feedback aimed at helping students improve specific skills.
Separate practice from performance	1. Provide opportunities for students to apply content and skills to concrete projects and activities.

- *Teaching about style* or helping students to understand their own reading strengths and weaknesses so that they can achieve the balance needed to become A+ readers

After the strategies for teaching to, with, and about style, we provide a set of style-based question stems and starters in each content area, and we demonstrate a strategy known as Force Field Analysis, designed specifically to work one-on-one with the students who struggle the most with reading.

Teaching to Students' Reading Styles

Teaching to students' styles means using reading styles as a support structure so that students have the opportunity to learn according to their strengths. Students who are weak in one or two styles may be missing out on essential learning because reading instruction so regularly focuses on their weak styles rather than

Figure 7.4. Guidelines for Working With Understanding Readers

Provide questions that puzzle and data that teases	1. Provide provocative questions that spur curiosity and focus students' attention on controversies or scholarly issues. 2. Use "Yes, but why?" inquiries to encourage students to probe more deeply. 3. Explore how reading is a form of problem solving.
Respond to student queries and provide reasons why	1. Establish purpose and reason for reading. 2. Allow students to generate their own questions before, during, and after reading. 3. Encourage students to generate not only what they know before a reading, but also what they think they know and want to know.
Open opportunities for critical thinking, problem solving, research projects, and debate	1. Use critical thinking strategies such as Compare and Contrast, Mystery, and Do You Hear What I Hear? to guide reading. 2. Structure units around inquiries, themes, and problems. 3. Allow students to conduct independent research around their interests. 4. Set up debate structures in which students explore controversies and scholarly issues in the readings or unit.
Build in opportunities for explanation and proof using objective data and evidence	1. Conduct Socratic Seminars. 2. Probe student explanations for reasons and evidence. 3. Seek alternative explanations and points of view. 4. Use thesis essays, debates, student inquiries, editorials, and the like to assess learning.
Evaluate content and process	1. Encourage students to reflect upon the content and their cognitive processes. 2. Help students convert their reflections into self-directed learning plans.

their preferred ones. Think about it: If a student is a predominantly Self-Expressive reader who loves to focus on imagery, "What if?" questions, and creative projects, how likely is it that he or she will be thwarted by reading instruction that focuses only on textbook reading and end-of-chapter questions? Or, on the flip side, how well would a Mastery reader, who seeks direction and clarity in reading instruction, do in an environment where unstructured project work is the rule? The fact is, all students need their styles to be validated in the classroom if we expect them to be engaged and productive. The payoff is that once students feel their styles are valued, they become willing to develop areas of weakness and, more generally, to stretch and grow as learners. The proof of this can be found in a number of research studies (Carbo, 1992; Dunn, Griggs, & Beasley, 1995; Hanson, Dewing, Silver, & Strong, 1991) demonstrating significant improvements in performance and motivation when teachers pay attention to students' styles.

The organizers shown in Figures 7.3 through 7.6 provide easy-to-remember guidelines for working with all four styles of readers, as well as examples of how to meet those guidelines in reading instruction.

Figure 7.5. Guidelines for Working With Self-Expressive Readers

Inspire students to use their imaginations and explore alternatives	1. Focus reading instruction around imaginative texts and let students apply what they learn. 2. Provide opportunities for journal writing. 3. Encourage students to make pre-reading predictions. 4. Allow students to explore content through metaphors and "What if?" questions. 5. Encourage the use of image-making as a tool for making inferences.
Model creative work so that students can examine models and establish criteria for assessment	1. Allow students to examine the work of experts and to generate assessment criteria for their own work. 2. Teach students how to extrapolate structures and techniques so they can apply author's "tricks" to their own written work. 3. Model creative reading processes like making predictions, visualizing, deep processing, and developing metaphors.
Allow students choice in demonstrating what they know and understand	1. Provide alternative activities, media, and learning opportunities for students to deepen their understanding and explore ideas not addressed directly by the text. 2. Use culminating assessment tasks that challenge both academic understanding and creative capacities. 3. Assess understanding through Task Rotation.
Give feedback, coach, and provide audiences for sharing work	1. Provide opportunities to share ideas, interpretations, and work and to obtain feedback from an audience. 2. Use a "coach, mini-lesson, revise for improved quality" teaching structure. 3. Organize cooperative coaching groups around students' shared interests.
Evaluate and assess performance according to established criteria	1. Provide or develop with students assessment rubrics that indicate what superior work looks like. 2. Encourage students to practice self-assessment. 3. Set up "quality circles" and peer feedback groups.

Teaching With Reading Styles

Teaching *to* students' styles means helping students overcome reading difficulties by delivering instruction and providing coaching that matches the student's style as a reader. Teaching *with* reading styles is a broader approach that accommodates all students' styles while also challenging them to work in the styles needing development. Because the ultimate goal of style-centered instruction is to help students achieve balance and flexibility by developing their capacities in all

Figure 7.6. Guidelines for Working With Interpersonal Readers

Try to personalize the content	1. Look for ways to activate students' prior knowledge about the reading. 2. Use personal hooks; connect students' life experiences to the reading. 3. Fold in group discussion, peer work, and direct interaction with students. 4. Provide time for journal writing.
Reinforce learning through support and positive feedback throughout the process	1. Make sure the environment is comfortable. 2. Encourage expression of personal feelings during the reading process. 3. Provide praise and constructive feedback regularly. 4. Organize cooperative reading groups around students' shared interests. 5. Provide modeling, coaching, and direct instruction.
Use the world outside the classroom to make current, real-world connections to content	1. Find and discuss real-world examples connected with the unit or reading. 2. Apply reading to current student concerns. 3. Fold in interviews, field trips, letter-writing, and community work whenever possible.
Select activities that build upon personal experiences and cooperative structures	1. Allow students to explore ethical and moral dilemmas and social issues related to content. 2. Use cooperative learning and peer practice activities. 3. Encourage discussions. 4. Try role playing as a learning strategy in which students act out the ideas and issues in their reading.
Take time to help establish personal goals, encourage reflection, and praise performance.	1. Remind students that reading is a personal journey. 2. Emphasize the role of reflection in helping students become better readers. 3. Hold conferences in which you help students develop personal learning plans.

four styles, we might think of the techniques in this section as instruction and assessment management systems because they make it easy for teachers to work with the entire class in all four styles.

Comprehension Menus

As we have seen, all texts operate on various levels and make multiple demands on a reader. Comprehension Menus help students manage this textual layering by helping them to develop their abilities to think about texts in all four

Figure 7.7. Menu for Developing Questions

Mastery questions ask students to:	**Interpersonal questions ask students to:**
Recall facts: • Who? What? Where? When? How? *Describe and retell:* • Can you describe how it works? • Can you retell or summarize what happened? *Sequence and rank:* • What are the steps? • What are the five most important ideas?	*Empathize and describe feelings:* • How would you feel if _____ happened to you? How do you think _____ felt? • What decision would you make? • Can you reflect on your own thoughts and feelings? • Can you reflect on your own learning and reading process? *Value and appreciate:* • Why is _____ important to you? • What's the value of _____? • Can you connect this to your own life? *Explore human-interest problems:* • How would you advise or console _____? • How would you help each side come to an agreement?
Understanding questions ask students to:	**Self-expressive questions ask students to:**
Make connections: • What are the similarities and differences? • What are the causes/effects? • How are the parts connected? *Interpret, infer, and prove:* • Why? Can you explain it? • Can you prove it? • What evidence supports your position? *Explore underlying meanings:* • What are the hidden assumptions? • What conclusions can you draw? • What does the author mean by _____? • Can you define a concept or idea?	*Explain metaphorically or symbolically:* • How is _____ like _____? • Develop a metaphor for _____. *Develop images, hypotheses, and predictions:* • What would happen if _____? • Can you imagine _____? What would it look like/be like? • Can you form a hypothesis or prediction? *Develop original products:* • Create a poem, icon, skit, or sculpture to represent _____.

SOURCE: Adapted with permission from Silver et al. (2000).

reading styles. To develop a Comprehension Menu, a teacher simply asks students to respond to at least four different questions, one in each style, according to the menu shown in Figure 7.7.

For example, a middle school Earth Science teacher developed the Comprehension Menu shown in Figure 7.8 for a textbook reading on types of rocks.

Task Rotation

A Task Rotation (Silver et al., 1996) also uses four-style questioning to help students develop a comprehensive understanding of the texts they read. The key difference between a Comprehension Menu and a Task Rotation lies in the scope of the responses students are asked to generate. Whereas Comprehension Menus tend to require brief responses and are usually applied to a single reading, Task Rotations go deeper, often uniting a range of texts across a unit with

Figure 7.8. Earth Science Comprehension Menu

Mastery	Interpersonal
Describe the process by which igneous, metamorphic, and sedimentary rocks form.	Which of these three types of rocks best reflects your personality? Why?
Understanding	**Self-Expressive**
What are the key similarities and differences between each type of rock?	Create a visual symbol or a hand gesture for each type that will help you remember the key differences among them.

more project-driven work. The separate tasks in a Task Rotation may be distributed throughout a unit. For instance, over the course of a unit on conic sections, students might be asked to sketch and label conic sections according to given equations (Mastery), work in pairs to assess their understanding and develop personal learning plans (Interpersonal), create mnemonic devices or jingles that help them remember the formulas that describe conic sections (Self-Expressive), and conduct research into the topic projectile motion, explaining in a report how physicists use conic sections (Understanding). Alternatively, tasks may be given all at once as a culminating assessment. The teacher may assign all four tasks, allow students to choose the tasks they wish to complete, or combine choice and assignment. Figure 7.9 shows one such culminating assessment, designed by an American History teacher, for a unit on the rise of industrialism (1865-1900).

Task Rotations can also be used to facilitate deep, multifaceted explorations of a single text. This approach is most common for texts that raise issues central to the discipline or that the teacher believes bear thorough examination. Figure 7.10 shows a Task Rotation based on an article on biological warfare.

Teaching Around the Wheel

The third approach to teaching with styles is called Teaching Around the Wheel (Silver & Hanson, 1998). Focused on instruction more than assessment, Teaching Around the Wheel means planning and delivering a series of instructional episodes in all four styles. By linking lesson planning to styles in this way, the teacher ensures that the learning and reading needs of all students are met. At the same time, the learning experience is enriched by styles: All students are challenged to master literal and factual information (Mastery), use critical thinking and interpretive skills (Understanding), explore and apply learning (Self-Expressive), and connect learning to their own lives and personal experiences (Interpersonal).

Figure 7.9. Task Rotation–Rise of Industrialism Assessment

Mastery	Interpersonal
Describe the five most important political and social developments. Justify your choices.	Who do you think best represents American values in this time period—the American farmer, the American worker, or the American entrepreneur? Justify/explain your choice.
Understanding	**Self-Expressive**
What was life like for the average American in 1840? What was it like for the average American in 1890? Was the average American better off in 1890 than he was in 1840? Prove your thesis. (Include specific reasons/proof.)	Create a representation/symbol of the American dream in 1840 and one for the American dream in 1890. Explain how each symbol characterizes the American dream in its period.

Figure 7.10. Task Rotation–Biological Warfare

Mastery	Interpersonal
Summarize the history of biological warfare.	Imagine you have been working with victims of biological weapons as part of a humanitarian group. Develop a brief speech you would deliver at the United Nations that makes clear the human toll these weapons take.
Understanding	**Self-Expressive**
Explain the relationship between government and science in the development of biological weapons. Who bears greater responsibility for the escalation of their development? Explain your answer using evidence from the text.	How would you go about solving the world crisis presented by biological weapons? Formulate a plan that involves the scientific community, industry, government, and the public at large.

Figure 7.11. Teaching Around the Wheel Lesson

Instructional Activity	Style
Colorful Impressions Read the first three chapters of *Lord of the Flies*. In your *Write to Learn* book, record your first impressions of the four major characters: Ralph, Jack, Piggy, and Simon. Select a color to represent your first impressions of each character and explain your choice of color.	M ___ U _x_ S ___ I _xx_
Matrix Organizer Make a character matrix to collect information about each of the four characters. Collect information about the physical characteristics and specific actions of each character.	M _xx_ U ___ S ___ I ___
Speculations Based on your observations, speculate about what is going on inside each character—what his feelings are and the motivations for his behavior.	M ___ U _xx_ S _x_ I _xx_
Character Sketch Select a piece of music or draw a sketch that represents the personality of each of the four characters based on your data and impressions. Include a written description with your picture or music.	M _x_ U ___ S ___ I _xx_
Predictions Based on your personality sketches, predict what the interaction between any two characters will be like. How will they react to each other and treat each other as the story unfolds? Be prepared to defend your ideas about their personality and their interactions in a group discussion.	M ___ U ___ S ___ I _xx_
Rank Order Ladder Of the four characters, which one is most like you? Which one is least like you? Rank the characters in descending order from most like to least like yourself. Give at least three reasons for each ranking.	M _x_ U _xx_ S ___ I ___
Metaphorical Expression *Choose: microscope, hammer, mirror, rope.* Use your choice to create an extended metaphor to describe one of the four characters in the text. Your essay should include a description of the character, a thesis statement that will be your metaphor, at least three reasons to support your analogy, and a conclusion. Share your essay with your writing group and obtain feedback on the depth of your understanding of the character, the strength of your metaphor, and your use of writing conventions.	M ___ U _x_ S _xx_ I _xx_

SOURCE: Adapted from Silver, Strong, and Hanson (2000).

Figure 7.11 shows a Teaching Around the Wheel lesson on the first three chapters of William Golding's *Lord of the Flies*. Notice how the teacher kept track of the styles each instructional episode enlisted (M = Mastery, U = Understanding, S = Self-Expressive, I = Interpersonal).

Teaching About Reading Styles

If we think of teaching *to* reading styles and teaching *with* reading styles as ways to support student learning and manage style-based instruction, respectively, then teaching *about* reading styles can be characterized as *helping students to understand and improve themselves as readers.* Research on the power of metacognition (Baker & Brown, 1984)—of teaching students how to pay attention to their own thinking processes—shows that when students understand their own strengths and weaknesses as learners (self-knowledge), they have an easier time determining what skills and strategies they will need to apply to particular texts or to perform specific tasks (task knowledge). Development of self-knowledge and task knowledge, in turn, leads to self-regulation—an ability possessed by all proficient readers that enables them to monitor their own comprehension and shift reading strategies when difficulties arise.

One of the simplest and most effective ways to build metacognition into reading instruction is to use an assessment instrument, such as the Reading Style Inventory (Strong & Silver, in press). The Reading Style Inventory contains thirty-six multiple-choice questions that ask students to consider the following:

- What motivates them as readers

- What they like to read

- How they approach reading before, during, and after the process

- What kinds of reading questions and projects they like and dislike

- How they address common reading difficulties

- What they look for from a reading teacher

The responses to each of the questions are keyed to the four learning styles. A sample set of items appears in Figure 7.12.

By assessing students' styles with the Reading Style Inventory, both the teacher and student get a comprehensive portrait of each student's preferences, strengths, and weaknesses as a reader. In this way, the instrument facilitates the personal reflections, conferences, and coaching sessions that lead to self-regulated reading.

Applications to Specific Content Areas

Developing Style-Based Questions in the Content Areas

Earlier in this chapter, we provided a menu of question stems and starters (see Figure 7.7) to help teachers create style-based questions. That menu was a general one, applicable to all content areas. In Figure 7.13, you will find a set of menus geared to social studies, math, science, and English, respectively. Although these menus are by no means comprehensive, they demonstrate how the specific content and types of texts found in each discipline lend themselves to examination through the lens of style.

Figure 7.12. Sample Excerpts From the Reading Style Inventory

I like books that 1. Teach me how to do or make something 2. Make me think 3. Help me understand other people 4. Create vivid pictures in my mind	When I'm reading, I tend to focus on 1. Ideas 2. Feelings 3. Images and patterns 4. Details
I am most comfortable reading texts that 1. Contain provocative ideas 2. Have characters I can identify with 3. Require me to use my imagination 4. Are clear and get to the point	After reading, I'm most likely to 1. Retell what I've read to myself 2. Reflect on my own emotional responses 3. Try to write something that's like what I've just read 4. Think about questions I have
As a reader, I tend to 1. Lose myself for hours when I'm interested 2. Make plans for reading 3. Read only when I want to or have to 4. Read a little bit every day	I like reading questions that ask 1. How I feel 2. What if? 3. Why? 4. What, where, who, when, or how?
Before reading, I 1. Look the text over to see how it's divided into sections 2. Determine the questions I want the text to answer 3. Predict what the text will be about 4. Think about how the text might be connected to my life	Reading causes me trouble when the language is 1. Too focused on details 2. Too abstract and complicated 3. Too full of emotions 4. Too poetic or unreal
	I like reading teachers who 1. Assign interesting reading projects 2. Lead exciting conversations about what a text means to us 3. Ask questions that force me to think and justify my ideas 4. Show me exactly what to do step-by-step

SOURCE: Strong and Silver (in press). Reprinted with permission.

Strategies for Struggling Readers

Using Force Field Analysis to Help Struggling Readers

Reading styles, by capitalizing on students' strengths and minimizing weaknesses, provide an ideal framework for working productively with struggling readers. One of the most intensive and personal ways to help a struggling reader is to use a style-based process known as Force Field Analysis. A Force Field Analysis entails plotting the positive and negative forces operating within a student's reading profile and then using that information to develop a prescriptive plan.

Figure 7.13. Question Menus in the Content Areas

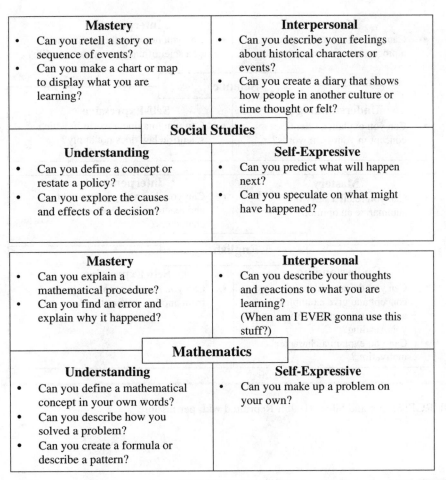

Mastery	Interpersonal
• Can you retell a story or sequence of events? • Can you make a chart or map to display what you are learning?	• Can you describe your feelings about historical characters or events? • Can you create a diary that shows how people in another culture or time thought or felt?

Social Studies

Understanding	Self-Expressive
• Can you define a concept or restate a policy? • Can you explore the causes and effects of a decision?	• Can you predict what will happen next? • Can you speculate on what might have happened?

Mastery	Interpersonal
• Can you explain a mathematical procedure? • Can you find an error and explain why it happened?	• Can you describe your thoughts and reactions to what you are learning? (When am I EVER gonna use this stuff?)

Mathematics

Understanding	Self-Expressive
• Can you define a mathematical concept in your own words? • Can you describe how you solved a problem? • Can you create a formula or describe a pattern?	• Can you make up a problem on your own?

(continued)

Steps for conducting a Force Field Analysis follow, along with a teacher's analysis and plan for a struggling reader named Mark:

1. Identify a student who is experiencing reading difficulty in your class.

> Mark is having a hard time in our short story unit.

2. Briefly describe, in writing, what you know about the student as a reader. Include the student's specific difficulties as you've diagnosed them. Also include what you know about the broader picture, including interests, talents, learning behaviors, and personality.

Figure 7.13. Continued

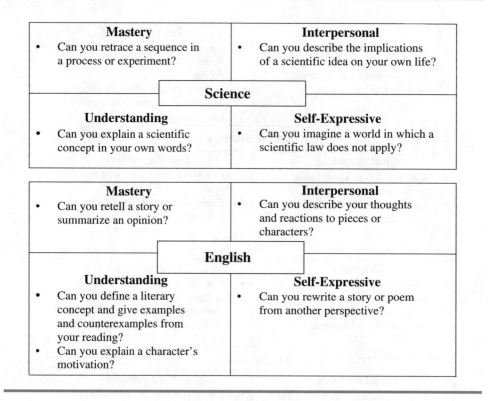

Mastery	Interpersonal
• Can you retrace a sequence in a process or experiment?	• Can you describe the implications of a scientific idea on your own life?

Science

Understanding	Self-Expressive
• Can you explain a scientific concept in your own words?	• Can you imagine a world in which a scientific law does not apply?

Mastery	Interpersonal
• Can you retell a story or summarize an opinion?	• Can you describe your thoughts and reactions to pieces or characters?

English

Understanding	Self-Expressive
• Can you define a literary concept and give examples and counterexamples from your reading? • Can you explain a character's motivation?	• Can you rewrite a story or poem from another perspective?

SOURCE: Strong and Silver (1996). Reprinted with permission.

Mark's main difficulties in reading short stories center on interpretation and critical analysis. He has a hard time separating his personal reaction from what the text actually conveys. When Mark is asked to provide support for his ideas, he usually says, "Because that's the way I feel," or "Because if I were so and so, that's what I would do." Similarly, Mark founders when it comes to finding textual evidence that illuminates the author's purpose or the major themes in a text.

In general, Mark is a classroom leader. He loves sharing his experiences and participating in discussions. He works well in groups and is caring, funny, and charismatic; as a result, some students look to him as a classroom mediator.

Outside of the classroom, Mark is a star athlete. He is captain of the freshman baseball team and also plays basketball and soccer.

3. Based on your description, identify what you believe to be the student's preferred reading style. Try to connect reading behaviors to the larger picture in determining the student's dominant style.

> Because Mark relates so personally to reading, it seems that he is an Interpersonal reader. His interest in personal experience, his love of group work and discussion, and his capacities as a leader and harmonizer all seem to verify this conclusion.

4. Compare your perceptions and observations with the results from the Reading Style Inventory.

> Results from the Reading Style Inventory:
>
> Most preferred: Interpersonal
>
> Second: Mastery
>
> Third: Self-Expressive
>
> Least preferred: Understanding
>
> These results match with my observations. Mark is a strong Interpersonal reader. He is also fairly strong in the Mastery style. His weakness in finding and using evidence correlates with the fact that the Understanding style is his weakest.

5. Based on your observations and the results from the Reading Style Inventory, use a Force Field Analysis to analyze the positive and negative forces operating in the student's profile.

Forces Working For	*Forces Working Against*
Likes to participate	Has trouble separating his personal reactions from the content
Works actively	Lacks objectivity
Works well in group or team activities	Is impulsive and sometimes careless
Is highly verbal	Is nonreflective
Has strong opinions	Has difficulty interpreting beyond the personal level
Is well-liked and respected	
Has strong physical nature	

6. Establish goals and objectives based on your analysis.

> Goal: To help Mark develop his analytical and interpretive abilities so that he is able to identify main ideas and important details, and so he can develop evidence-based interpretations

7. Develop a plan for potential activities and teaching strategies. The goal here is to tap into the student's strengths while developing areas of weakness (see Figure 7.14).

Figure 7.14. Potential Activities and Teaching Strategies Chart

---

1. *Interview:* Have Mark assess his strengths and weaknesses in reading. Ask him what he believes good readers do when they read. Together, identify behaviors that will support Mark's learning.

   > Taps into: Need to work with others, verbal nature
   > Develops: Ability to reflect, objectivity, ability to curtail impulsivity

2. *Split-Screen Note Making and Graphic Organizers:* Model how to use sketches, drawings, and concept maps to capture main ideas.

   > Taps into: Active learning, physical nature (drawing)
   > Develops: Ability to interpret beyond personal level

3. *Work with an Understanding Reader:* Working with a student whose strengths match his weaknesses, Mark should learn to use a main idea organizer to find big ideas and supporting details.

   > Taps into: Need for group/team learning
   > Develops: Interpreting beyond personal level, ability to reflect, objectivity

4. *Personalize content:* Ask Mark, "What if you were an idea and wanted to become a main idea. How would you make yourself stand out from the rest of the ideas?"

   > Taps into: Need for personal connection
   > Develops: Ability to reflect, ability to begin moving beyond the personal

5. *Use evidence for everyday activities:* To help Mark internalize the thesis-evidence structure, ask him to provide evidence for and against statements such as "It is easier to take care of a plant than a pet."

   > Taps into: Need for personal connection
   > Develops: Ability to interpret beyond personal level

6. *Collaborative Summarizing:* Read text aloud first and ask students to listen. Students then reread the text and, in groups, develop a collaborative summary. Each student identifies what he/she believes are the three to five most important points. Groups negotiate their lists until all agree on the same points. Then they write a summary together.

   > Taps into: Need for group work
   > Develops: Ability to interpret beyond personal level

7. *Reciprocal Teaching Journals:* Have Mark use a Reciprocal Teaching Journal to ask questions, think about vocabulary, make predictions, and summarize thoughts before he shares ideas. Read regularly and provide feedback. Emphasize importance of thinking ideas through before speaking.

   > Taps into: Need for personal connection
   > Develops: Ability to reflect, ability to curtail impulsivity

References

■ ■

Adler, M. (1982). The paideia proposal: Rediscovering the essence of education. *American School Board Journal, 169*(7), 17-20.

Afflerbach, P. P., & Johnson, P. H. (1986). *What do expert readers do when the main idea is not explicit?* In J. F. Baumann (Ed.), *Teaching main idea comprehension* (pp. 49-72). Newark, DE: International Reading Association.

Baker, L., & Brown, A. (1984). Cognitive monitoring in reading. In J. Flood (Ed.), *Understanding reading comprehension* (pp. 21-44). Newark, DE: International Reading Association.

Beck, I. L., & Carpenter, P. A. (1986). Cognitive approaches to understanding reading: Implications for instructional practice. *American Psychologist, 41*(10), 1098-1105.

Beck, I. L., McKeown, M. G., Hamilton, R. L., & Kucan, L. (1997). *Questioning the author: An approach for enhancing student engagement with text.* Newark, DE: International Reading Association.

Bloom, B. (Ed.). (1956). *Taxonomy of education objectives, the classification of educational goals: Handbook I. Cognitive domain.* New York: David McKay.

Briggs, K. C., & Myers, I. B. (1998). Myers-Briggs Type Indicator ®, Form M. Palo Alto, CA: Consulting Psychologists Press. (Original work published 1962)

Brooks, J. G., & Brooks, M. G. (1999). *In search of understanding: The case for constructivist classrooms.* Alexandria, VA: Association for Supervision and Curriculum Development.

Brown, A. L. (1989). Analogical learning and transfer: What develops? In I. S. Vosniador & A. Ortony (Eds.), *Similarity and analogical reasoning.* Cambridge, MA: Cambridge University Press.

Brownlie, F., Close, S., & Wingren, L. (1990). *Tomorrow's classrooms today: Strategies for creating active readers, writers, and thinkers.* Markham, Ontario, Canada: Pembroke.

Brownlie, F., & Silver, H. F. (1995a, January). *Effective notemaking strategies.* Paper presented at the seminar "Responding Thoughtfully to the Challenge of Diversity," Delta School District Conference, Delta, British Columbia, Canada.

Brownlie, F., & Silver, H. F. (1995b, January). *Mind's eye.* Paper presented at the seminar "Responding Thoughtfully to the Challenge of Diversity," Delta School District Conference Center, Delta, British Columbia, Canada.

Bruer, J. T. (1993). *Schools for thought: A science of learning in the classroom.* Cambridge: MIT Press.

Bruner, J. S. (1957). Going beyond the information given. In J. S. Bruner, E. Brunswick, L. Festinger, F. Heider, K. F. Muenzinger, D. E. Osgood, & D. Rapaport (Eds.), *Contemporary approaches to cognition.* Cambridge, MA: Harvard University Press.

Carbo, M. (1992, January-February). Giving unequal learners an equal chance: A reply to a biased critique of learning styles. *Remedial & Special Education, 13*(1), 19-29.

173

Carson, J. G., Chase, N. D., Gibson, S. U., & Hargrove, M. F. (1992). Literacy demands of the undergraduate curriculum. *Reading, Research, and Instruction, 31,* 25-30.

Costa, A. R. (1991). Teacher behaviors that enable student thinking. In *Developing minds* (Vol. 1, rev. ed.). Alexandria, VA: Association for Supervision and Curriculum Development.

Derewianka, B. (1990). *Exploring how texts work.* Newtown, Australia: Primary English Teaching Association.

Dickson, S. V. (1995). Instruction in expository text: A focus on compare/contrast structure. *LD Forum, 20*(2), 8-15.

Dunn, R., Griggs, S. A., & Beasley, M. (1995, July). A meta-analytic validation of the Dunn and Dunn model of learning style preferences. *Journal of Educational Research, 88*(6), 353-362.

Escondido School District. (1979). *Mind's eye.* Escondido, CA: Escondido Board of Education.

Fry, E. (1981). Graphical literacy. *Journal of Reading, 24,* 383-390.

Gambrell, L. B., & Bales, R. J. (1986). Mental imagery and the comprehension-monitoring performance of fourth- and fifth-grade poor readers. *Reading Research Quarterly, 21,* 454-464.

Gardner, H. (1983). *Frames of mind: The theory of multiple intelligences.* New York: Basic Books.

Gardner, H. (1999). *Intelligence reframed: Multiple intelligences for the 21st century.* New York: Basic Books.

Hanson, J. R., Dewing, T., Silver, H. F., & Strong, R. W. (1991). Within our reach: Identifying and working more effectively with at-risk learners. In *Students At-Risk* (Produced for the 1991 ASCD Conference, San Francisco, CA). Alexandria, VA: Association for Supervision and Curriculum Development.

Herber, H. (1970). *Teaching reading in the content areas.* Englewood Cliffs, NJ: Prentice Hall.

Herrman, B. A. (1992). Teaching and assessing strategic reasoning: Dealing with the dilemmas. *Reading Teacher, 45*(6), 428-433.

Hoffman, J. V. (1992). Critical reading/thinking across the curriculum: Using I-charts to support learning. *Language Arts, 69,* 121-127.

Jenkins, J. R., Stein, M. L., & Wysocki, K. (1984). Learning vocabulary through reading. *American Educational Research Journal, 21*(4), 767-787.

Johnson, D. W., & Johnson, R. T. (1999*). Learning together and alone: Cooperative, competitive, and individualistic learning.* Boston: Allyn & Bacon.

Johnson, D., Maruyama, G., Johnson, R., Nelson, D., & Skon, L. (1981). Effects of cooperative, competitive, and individualistic goal structures on achievement: A meta-analysis. *Psychological Bulletin, 89*(1), 47-62.

Jung, C. (1923). *Psychological types* (trans. H. G. Baynes). New York: Harcourt, Brace.

Just, M. A., & Carpenter, P. A. (1987). *The psychology of reading and language comprehension.* Rockleigh, NJ: Allyn & Bacon.

Keene, E. O., & Zimmerman, S. (1997). *Mosaic of thought: Teaching comprehension in a reader's workshop.* Portsmouth, NH: Heinemann.

Kierwa, K. A. (1985). Student's note-taking behaviors and the efficacy of providing the instructor's notes for review. *Contemporary Educational Psychology, 10,* 378-386.

Knudson, R. E. (1989). *Teaching children to write: Informal writing* (Research report; materials developed from PhD thesis, *Effects of Instructional Strategies in Student Writing*). (ERIC Document Reproduction Service No. ED 310 425)

Lake, J. H. (1973). *The influence of wait-time on the verbal dimension of student inquiry behavior.* Doctoral dissertation, Rutgers University, New Brunswick, NJ.

Martin-Kniep, G. O. (2000). *Becoming a better teacher: Eight innovations that work.* Alexandria, VA: Association for Supervision and Curriculum Development.

Marzano, R. J. (1992). *A different kind of classroom: Teaching with dimensions of learning*. Alexandria, VA: Association for Supervision and Curriculum Development.

Marzano, R. J., Brandt, R. S., Hughes, C. S., Jones, B. F., Presseisen, B. Z., Rankin, S. C., & Sukor, C. (1988). *Dimensions of thinking: A framework for curriculum and instruction*. Alexandria, VA: Association for Supervision and Curriculum Development.

Marzano, R. J., Gaddy, B. B., & Dean, C. (2000). *What works in classroom instruction*. Aurora, CO: Mid-continent Research for Education and Learning.

McGilly, K. (Ed.). (1994). *Classroom lessons: Integrating cognitive theory and classroom practice*. Cambridge: MIT Press.

McKenzie, G. (1979). Data charts: A crutch for helping pupils organize reports. *Language Arts, 56,* 784, 788.

Mullis, I. V. S., Owen, G. H., & Phillips, G. W. (1990). *America's challenge: Accelerating academic achievement (a summary of findings from 20 years of NAEP)*. Princeton, NJ: Educational Testing Service.

Muth, D. K. (1987). Structure strategies for comprehending expository text. *Reading Research and Instruction, 27*(1), 66-72.

Ogle, D. (1986). K-W-L: A teaching model that develops active reading of the expository text. *The Reading Teacher, 39,* 564-570.

Osman-Jouchoux, R. (1997). Linking reading and writing: Concept mapping as an organizing tactic. In R. E. Griffin, J. M. Hunter, C. B. Schiffman, & W. J. Gibbs (Eds.), *Vision quest: Journeys toward visual literacy* (1996 conference). Corsicana, TX: International Visual Literacy Association.

Paivio, A. (1990). *Mental representations: A dual coding approach*. New York: Oxford University Press.

Palinscar, A. S., & Brown, A. L. (1984). Reciprocal teaching of comprehension-monitoring activities. *Cognition and Instruction, 1*(2), 117-175.

Pauk, W. (1974). *How to study in college*. Boston: Houghton Mifflin.

Pearson, P. D., & Comperell, K. (1994). Comprehension of text structures. In R. B. Ruddell, H. Singer, & M. R. Ruddell (Eds.), *Theoretical models and processes of reading* (4th ed., pp. 448-468). Newark, DE: International Reading Assocation.

Pressley, M. (1977). Imagery and children's learning: Putting the picture in developmental perspective. *Review of Educational Research, 47,* 586-622.

Pressley, M., Woloshyn, V., & Associates. (1995). *Cognitive strategy instruction that really improves children's academic performance*. Cambridge, MA: Brookline.

Reid, L. (1983). *Talking: The neglected part of the writing process*. Paper presented at the Annual Meeting of the National Council of Teachers of English, Spring Conference, Seattle, WA.

Reinking, D. (1986). Integrating graphic aids into content area instruction: The graphic information lesson. *Journal of Reading, 30,* 146-151.

Rowe, M. B. (1972). *Wait-time and rewards as instructional variables: Their influence on language, logic, and fate control*. Paper presented at the National Association for Research in Science Teaching, Chicago, IL.

Sadoski, M. (1985). The natural use of imagery in story comprehension and recall: Replication and extension. *Reading Research Quarterly, 19,* 110-123.

Siegel, M. G. (1984). *Reading as signification*. Doctoral dissertation, Indiana University, Bloomington.

Silver, H. F., & Hanson, J. R. (1998). *Learning styles and strategies* (3rd ed.). Woodbridge, NJ: Thoughtful Education Press.

Silver, H. F., Hanson, J. R., Strong, R. W., & Schwartz, P. B. (1996). *Teaching styles and strategies* (3rd ed.). Trenton, NJ: Thoughtful Education Press.

Silver, H. F., & Strong, R. W. (1994). *Reading styles and strategies* (workshop ed.) Trenton, NJ: Thoughtful Education Press.

Silver, H. F., Strong, R. W., & Hanson, R. J. (2000). *Learning preference inventory: User's manual.* Trenton, NJ: Thoughtful Education Press.

Silver, H. F., Strong, R. W., & Perini, M. J. (2000). *Reading for meaning: The teaching strategies library.* Trenton, NJ: Thoughtful Education Press.

Silver, H. F., Strong, R. W., & Perini, M. J. (2001). *Tools for promoting active, in-depth learning* (2nd ed.). Trenton, NJ: Thoughtful Education Press.

Silver, H. F., Strong, R. W., & Perini, M. J. (in press). *Concept attainment.* Trenton, NJ: Thoughtful Education Press.

Song, M. (1998). *Experimental study of the effect of controlled vs. freewriting and different feedback types on writing quality and writing apprehension of EFL college students.* South Korea. (ERIC Document Reproduction Service No. ED 423 703)

Sparks, J. E. (1982). *Write for power.* Los Angeles: Communication Associates.

Stahl, S. A., & Fairbanks, M. M. (1986). The effects of vocabulary instruction: A model-based meta-analysis. *Review of Educational Research, 56*(1), 72-110.

Sternberg, R. J. (1985). *Beyond I.Q.: A triarchic theory of human intelligence.* New York: Cambridge University Press.

Sternberg, R. J. (1999). The nature of mathematical reasoning. In L. V. Stiff & F. R. Curcio (Eds.), *Developing mathematical reasoning in grades K-12: 1999 Yearbook.* Reston, VA: National Council of Teachers of Mathematics.

Strong, R. W., Hanson, J. R., & Silver, H. F. (1995). *Questioning styles and strategies* (2nd ed.). Woodbridge, NJ: Thoughtful Education Press.

Strong, R. W., & Silver, H. F. (1996). *An introduction to thoughtful curriculum and assessment.* Trenton, NJ: Thoughtful Education Press.

Strong, R. W., & Silver, H. F. (1998a). Math styles and strategies (workshop ed.). Woodbridge, NJ: Thoughtful Education Press.

Strong, R. W., & Silver, H. F. (1998b). *Simple and deep: Factors affecting classroom implementation and student performance.* Unpublished research.

Strong, R. W., & Silver, H. F. (in press). *The reading style inventory.* Trenton, NJ: Thoughtful Education Press.

Suchman, J. R. (1966). *Developing inquiry.* Chicago: Science Research Associates.

Taba, H. (1971). *Hilda Taba teaching strategies program.* Miami, FL: Institute for Staff Development.

Thomas, E. (1999). *Styles and strategies for teaching high school mathematics.* Trenton, NJ: Thoughtful Education Press.

Tierney, R. J., & Shanahan, T. (1991). Research on reading-writing relationships: Interactions, transactions, and outcomes. In P. D. Pearson, R. Barr, M. Kamil, & P. Mosenthal (Eds.), *Handbook of reading research* (2nd ed., pp. 246-280). New York: Longman.

Vacca, R. T., & Vacca, J. L. (1998). *Content area reading: Literacy and learning across the curriculum.* New York: Longman.

Veit, R. (1981). *Creating conditions for learning: A further argument for free writing.* Paper presented at the Annual Meeting of the Conference on College Composition and Communication, Dallas, TX.

Walberg, H. J. (1999). Productive teaching. In H. C. Waxman & H. J. Walberg (Eds.), *New directions for teaching practice and research* (pp. 75-104). Berkeley, CA: McCutchen.

Wiggins, G., & McTighe, J. (1998). *Understanding by design.* Alexandria, VA: Assocation for Supervision and Curriculum Development.

Williams, A. P. (1992). *A comparison between the reading comprehension of eleventh grade students who incorporate free writing exercises into their literature class and those eleventh grade students who do not incorporate free writing into their literature class.* McKeesport, PA: McKeesport Area School District.

Wood, K. (1986). The effect of interspersing questions in text: Evidence for "slicing the task." *Reading Research & Instruction, 25,* 295-307.

Woodward, A., & Elliott, D. L. (1990). Textbook use and teacher professionalism. In D. L. Elliott & A. Woodward (Eds.), *Textbooks and Schooling in the U.S.* (89th Yearbook of the National Society for the Study of Education, Part 1, pp. 178-193). Chicago: National Society for the Study of Education.

Zeiderman, H. (1994). *Investigating mathematics: The touchstones approach.* Annapolis, MD: C. Z. M.

Zeiderman, H. (1995). *A guide for leading discussions using Touchstones Volume I: Touchstones teachers guide Volume I.* Annapolis, MD: C. Z. M.

Index

CORWIN
PRESS

The Corwin Press logo—a raven striding across an open book—represents the happy union of courage and learning. We are a professional-level publisher of books and journals for K–12 educators, and we are committed to creating and providing resources that embody these qualities. Corwin's motto is "Success for All Learners."